S0-EXB-768

WITHDRAWN

For Reference

Not to be taken from this room

Seal of the State of New Hampshire

CHRONOLOGY AND DOCUMENTARY HANDBOOK OF THE STATE OF
NEW HAMPSHIRE

ROBERT I. VEXLER

State Editor

WILLIAM F. SWINDLER

Series Editor

1978 OCEANA PUBLICATIONS, INC./Dobbs Ferry, New York

Library of Congress Cataloging in Publication Data
Main entry under title:

Chronology and documentary handbook of the State of
   New Hampshire.

   (Chronologies and documentary handbooks of the States;
29)
   Bibliography: p.
   Includes Index.
   SUMMARY: Contains a chronology of historical events
from 1498 to 1977, a biographical directory of prominent
citizens, and selected documents including the State
constitutions of 1776 and 1784.
   1. New Hampshire—History—Chronology. 2. New
Hampshire—Biography. 3. New Hampshire—History—

Sources. [1. New Hampshire—History] I. Vexler,
Robert I. II. Series.
F34.5.C46   974.2′002′02   78-16165
ISBN 0-379-16154-0

© Copyright 1978 by Oceana Publications, Inc.

All rights reserved. No part of this publication may be reproduced or transmitted in any form or by any means, electronic or mechanical, including photocopy, recording, xerography, or any information storage and retrieval system, without permission in writing from the publisher.

Manufactured in the United States of America

TABLE OF CONTENTS

INTRODUCTION ix

CHRONOLOGY (1498-1977) 1

BIOGRAPHICAL DIRECTORY 21

PROMINENT PERSONALITIES 49

FIRST STATE CONSTITUTIONS 55
    Constitution of 1776 57
    Constitution of 1784 59

SELECTED DOCUMENTS 73
    The Condition of New Hampshire -- 1730/1 75
    Robert Rogers, "The Ranger," and His Descendants 79
    Portsmouth's Old Homes 83
    Glimpses of an Old Social Capital 89
    New Hampshire and the Federal Judiciary, 1794-1795 95
    Whittier's New Hampshire 99
    The White Mountains 107
    New Hampshire in the 20th Century 111
    Basic Facts 137
    Map of Congressional Districts 139

SELECTED BIBLIOGRAPHY 141

NAME INDEX 145

ACKNOWLEDGMENT

Special recognition should be accorded Melvin Hecker, whose research has made a valuable contribution to this volume.

Thanks to my wife, Francine, in appreciation of her help in the preparation of this work.

Thanks also to my children, David and Melissa, without whose patience and understanding I would have been unable to devote the considerable time necessary for completing the state chronology series.

Robert I. Vexler

INTRODUCTION

This projected series of <u>Chronologies and Documentary Handbooks of the States</u> will ultimately comprise fifty separate volumes - one for each of the states of the Union. Each volume is intended to provide a concise ready reference of basic data on the state, and to serve as a starting point for more extended study as the individual user may require. Hopefully, it will be a guidebook for a better informed citizenry - students, civic and service organizations, professional and business personnel, and others.

The editorial plan for the <u>Handbook</u> series falls into six divisions: (1) a chronology of selected events in the history of the state; (2) a short biographical directory of the principal public officials, e.g., governors, Senators and Representatives; (3) a short biographical directory of prominent personalities of the state (for most states); (4) the first state constitution; (5) the text of some representative documents illustrating main currents in the political, economic, social or cultural history of the state; and (6) a selected bibliography for those seeking further or more detailed information. Most of the data found in the present volume, in fact, have been taken from one or another of these references.

The current constitutions of all fifty states, as well as the federal Constitution, are regularly kept up to date in the definitive collection maintained by the Legislative Drafting Research Fund of Columbia University and published by the publisher of the present series of <u>Handbooks</u>. These texts are available in most major libraries under the title, <u>Constitutions of the United States: National and State</u>, in two volumes, with a companion volume, the <u>Index Digest of State Constitutions</u>.

Finally, the complete collection of documents illustrative of the constitutional development of each state, from colonial or territorial status up to the current constitution as found in the Columbia University collection, is being prepared for publication in a multi-volume series by the present series editor. Whereas the present series of <u>Handbooks</u> is intended for a wide range of interested citizens, the series of annotated constitutional materials in the volumes of <u>Sources and Documents of U. S. Constitutions</u> is primarily for the specialist in government, history or law. This is not to suggest that the general citizenry may not profit equally from referring to these materials; rather, it points up the separate purpose of the <u>Handbooks</u>, which

ix

is to guide the user to these and other sources of authoritative information with which he may systematically enrich his knowledge of this state and its place in the American Union.

>William F. Swindler
>Series Editor
>
>Robert I. Vexler
>Series Associate Editor

Live Free or Die
State Motto

CHRONOLOGY

1498   John Cabot came to New England.

1501   Coterreal came to New England.

1603   Martin Pring visited the mouth of the Piscataqua River with the Speedwell and the Discoverer.

1605   Samuel de Champlain discovered the Isles of Shoals and sailed along the New Hampshire coast.

1620   The Council for New England was formed under the leadership of Sir Ferdinando Gorges.

1622   March 9. John Mason was granted the land between the Salem and Merrimac rivers. It was called Mariana.

             John Mason and Sir Ferdinando Gorges were jointly given the area between the Merrimac and Kennebec rivers for 60 miles. It was given the name of the Province of Maine.

             David Thomason and his associates were granted 6,000 acres near the mouth of the Piscataqua River.

1623   David Thomson established the first settlement in New Hampshire at Little Harbor. It is now called Rye. Dover was also founded at this time.

1628   March 19. Sir Henry Roswell and his associates received a grant of land three miles south of the Charles River to 3 miles north of the Kennebec River, extending west to the South Sea or Pacific Ocean. It was called Massachusetts.

1629   November 8. John Mason was given that part of Maine between the Merrimac and the Piscataqua Rivers, called New Hampshire.

             November 17. The Laconia Company, which was composed of Sir Ferdinando Gorges, John Mason and associates, received a grant of territory around the Lake of the Iroquois (Lake Champlain) and an additional 1,000 acres at some other place along the sea coast.

1630   March 12. Edward Hilton was given a grant

of land around the lower part of Dover Neck.

1631   November. The Laconia Company received a grant of land on both sides of the Piscataqua River, near its mouth. It was known as the Pescataway grant.

1635   April 22. John Mason was given a grant of land between the Salem River on the south and the Piscataqua and Salmon Falls rivers on the northeast. It also extended 60 miles inland. This grant was called New Hampshire.

1638   Rev. John Wheelwright, an Antimonian leader who had been exiled from Massachusetts, founded Exeter on the land which he claimed to have bought from the Indians.

1639   July 14. Wheelwright's settlers signed the Exeter Compact.

1640   Estimated population: 1,055.

1641   October 9. The residents of the four towns of Portsmouth, Dover, Hampton and Exeter submitted to the jurisdiction of Massachusetts.

1642   Hampton sumitted to the jurisdiction of Massachusetts.

1643   Exeter sumitted to the jurisdiction of Massachusetts.

1644   King Charles I appointed a commission which decided that Richard Mason's lands were not within the jurisdiction of Massachusetts.

1650   Estimated population: 1,305.

1660   Estimated population: 1,555.

1662   The selectmen of Portsmouth voted to establish some device in which to place people who slept or took tobacco on Sunday.

1670   Estimated population: 1,805.

1674   Richard Tufton Mason agreed to surrender his rights to the Crown in return for one-third of the customs, rents, fines and other

	profits derived therefrom, but the offer was refused.
1679	September 8. New Hampshire was made a separate royal colony. This had been arranged by Richard Tufton Mason, heir of John Mason, who had received the original grant. The squatters refused to leave the land, however.
	John Catt became president of the council which was to govern New Hampshire. He served in this capacity until 1681.
1680	Estimated population: 2,047.
1681	Richard Waldron became president of the council of New Hampshire. He served in this position until 1682.
1682	Edward Cranfield became lieutenant-governor of the Province. He served in this capacity until 1685.
1685	Walter Barefoot became deputy-governor of New Hampshire and served until 1686.
1686	New Hampshire became a part of the Dominion of New England. Joseph Dudley became president of the Council for New England and served in this office until 1687.
1687	Sir Edmund Andros became governor-general of New England and served until 1689.
1689	New Hampshire was nominally without a government. This condition continued for a short while until 1690.
	The Indians attacked Dover, killing Major Richard Waldron whom they believed had betrayed them some 13 years earlier.
1690	Estimated population: 4,164.
	New Hampshire, was nominally united with Massachusetts and continued until 1692.
1691	The Masons sold their land claims to Samuel Allen for ₺2,750. King William IV made Allen governor and commander in chief of New Hampshire, but he was not able to control the lands because juries found for the

residents.

1692　Samuel Allen became governor of the Province. He continued to serve until 1698.

1699　Richard Coote, the earl of Bellamont, became governor of the Province and continued in this capacity until 1701.

1700　Estimated population: 4,958.

1702　Joseph Dudley became governor of the Province of New Hampshire. He continued in the office until 1715.

1710　Estimated population: 5,681.

1716　Samuel Shute became governor of the Province. He continued to serve until 1723.

1720　Estimated population: 9,375.

1723　John Wentworth became lieutenant-governor of the province and ruled New Hampshire until 1728.

1729　William Burnett became governor of New Hampshire and served until 1730.

1730　Estimated population: 10,755

Jonathan Belcher became governor of New Hampshire and served in this capacity until 1741.

1737　A royal order referred the Massachusetts-New Hampshire border dispute to a commission, composed of councillors from New York, Nova Scotia, and Rhode Island. The commission agreed upon the present eastern boundary, but could not reach any conclusion concerning the southern boundary.

1740　Estimated population: 23,256.

Three families from Massachusetts began a settlement at Charlestown, the site of Fort Numberk.

1741　Benning Wentworth became governor of New Hampshire and continued to serve in this capacity until 1767.

CHRONOLOGY 5

1750	Estimated population: 27,505.
1754	August 30. Indians attacked James Johnson's house, which was near Fort Numberk. The family and their guests were taken captive. They were eventually brought to Montreal and sold. An arrangement was made for an exchange of prisoners in 1757. Mrs. Johnson was able to return to America. Mr. Johnson joined her in 1758.
1756	The first paper published in New Hampshire appeared at Portsmouth -- the _New Hampshire Gazette_.
1760	Estimated population: 39,093.
1766	John Wentworth became governor of New Hampshire and served during the year.
1767	John Wentworth became governor of the Province of New Hampshire again and served until 1775.
1769	April 29. The following counties were established: Cheshire, Grafton, Hillsborough, Rockingham, and Stratford. Cheshire, with its seat at Keene, was named for Cheshire County, England.

Grafton, with its seat at Woodsville, was named for Augustus Henry Fitzroy, third duke of Grafton, England's secretary of state for the northern department.

Hillsborough, with its seats at Nashua and Manchester, was named for Wills Hill, Earl of Hillsborough, a councillor of King George III and secretary of state for the colonies.

Rockingham, with its seat at Exeter, was named for Charles Watson Wentworth, second Marquis of Rockingham, Prime Minister of Great Britain when the Stamp Act was repealed.

Strafford, with its seat at Dover, was named for Thomas Wentworth, the earl of Strafford, leader in the House of Commons. |
| 1769 | Dartmouth College was opened in Hanover. |

1770	Estimated population: 62,396.
	George Whitefield, evangelist, died in New Hampshire.
1774	December 11-12. A group of patriots captured the British Fort William and Mary in Portsmouth. They took 100 barrels of gunpowder, 15 cannon and various other munitions. John Sullivan led the men. No serious casualties occurred.
1775	Matthew Thornton became president of the Provinical Convention.
1776	January 5. The first state constitution was adopted by the provincial congress. Although the constitution was to be temporary, it remained in effect until June 1784.
	June 15. The New Hampshire assembly voted for independence from Great Britain.
	Mesteck Weare became State President and served in this capacity until 1785.
1777	August 16. New Hampshire and Vermont troops under the command of General John Stark won the Battle of Bennington against the British troops.
1778	The College Party at Hanover gained support from 16 towns on the New Hampshire side of the river. They tried to convince them that they owed no allegiance to the new provincial government at Exeter. They would join the towns on the Vermont side of the Connecticut River.
1779	February. Vermont rejected the 16 New Hampshire towns.
1780	Estimated population: 87,802.
1781	Vermont claimed New Hampshire's valley towns. When the offer was made to admit Vermont as the 14th state in 1782, the latter returned the towns, but she was not admitted.
	Phillips Exeter Academy was founded.
1784	A new state constitution was adopted.

CHRONOLOGY

1785   John Landon became state president and served until 1786.

1786   General John Sullivan became state president and served until 1787.

General John Sullivan was able to prevent anarchy when 200 men marched into Exeter and surrounded the assembly. The mob demanded that the legislature provide paper money, but the state senate refused to act until the mob dispersed. General Sullivan called out the militia, and after a short skirmish, the mob broke up.

1788   February 13. The New Hampshire convention met at Exeter to consider the United States Constitution. They adjourned after ten days.

June 17. The New Hampshire convention reassembled at Concord after the recess.

June 21. The New Hampshire Constitutional Convention ratified the United States Constitution, becoming the 9th state to do so. The convention proposed 12 amendments.

1789   John Sullivan, Federalist, became state president. He served until 1790.

1790   Population: 141,885.

January 25. The state legislature ratified the first ten amendments to the United States Constitution, the Bill of Rights.

Josiah Bartlett, Democrat-Republican, became state president. He served until 1792.

1792   Josiah Bartlett, Federalist, became governor of the state and continued in office until 1794.

1794   June 16. The state legislature ratified the 11th Amendment to the United States Constitution.

Joseph Taylor Gilman, Federalist, became governor of the state and served in the office until 1805.

Portsmouth businessmen indicated their opposition to John Jay's Treaty which forbade large ships from trading with Great Britain or her dependencies.

1800   Population: 183,858

1803   December 24. Coos County, with its seat at Lancaster, was established. It became effective March 1, 1805.

The first cotton factory in the state was opened at New Ipswich.

1804   June 15. The state legislature ratified the 12th Amendment to the United States Constitution.

1805   John Langdon, Democrat-Republican, became governor of the state and served in the office until 1809.

1809   Jeremiah Smith, Federalist, became governor of the state and served in this capacity until 1810.

1810   Population: 214,460.

John Langdon, Democrat-Republican, again became governor of the state and served in the office until 1812.

1812   William Plumer, Democrat-Republican, became governor of New Hampshire and served in the office until 1813.

1813   John Taylor Gilman, Federalist, again became governor of the state and served in the office until 1816.

1816   William Plumer, Democrat-Republican, became governor of the state again and continued to serve in the office until 1819.

Samuel Bell, Democrat-Republican, became governor of New Hampshire and served in the office until 1823.

1819   February 2. The United States Supreme Court ruled in the case of <u>Trustees of Dartmouth College v. Woodward</u> that a charter granted to a private corporation is considered a contract. It is therefore protected under the United States Constitution against impairment by state legislatures. Therefore the New Hampshire law which created a state college out of Dartmouth was invalid.

The state legislature passed a toleration law which ended state support for the Congregational Church.

1820   Population: 244,161.

New Hampshire established one of the first state supported libraries in the United States along with New York.

1823   July 1. Merrimack County, with its seat at Concord, was established, effective August 1, 1823.

Levi Woodbury, Democrat-Republican, became governor of the state and served in the office until 1824.

1824   David Lawrence Morrill, Democrat-Republican, became governor of the state and served in office until 1827.

1827   July 5. Sullivan County, with Newport as its seay, was created, effective September, 1827. It was named for John Sullivan, member of the Continental Congress, major general in the Revolutionary War, President of New Hampshire, and speaker of the New Hampshire house of representatives.

Benjamin Pierce, Democrat-Republican, became governor of the state, and served in the office until 1828.

1828   John Bell, National Republican, became governor of New Hampshire. He served in the office until 1829.

1829   Benjamin Pierce, Jackson Democrat, again became governor of the state. He served in the office until 1830.

1830   Population: 269,328.

Matthew Harvey, Jackson Democrat, became governor and served until his resignation in 1831.

1831	May 23. Levi Woodbury became Secretary of the Navy in the Cabinet of President Andrew Jackson.

Joseph Morrill Harper, Democrat, became acting governor of the state.

Samuel Dinsmoor, Jackson Democrat, became governor of the state and served in this capacity until 1834. |
| 1834 | June 27. Levi Woodbury became Secretary of the Treasury in the Cabinet of President Andrew Jackson.

William Badger, Democrat, became governor of the state and served in the office until 1836. |
1836	Isaac Hill, Democrat, became governor of New Hampshire and served in this capacity until 1839.
1838	The first railroad was built in the state.
1839	John Page, Democrat, became governor of the state and served in the office until 1842.
1840	Population: 284,574.

December 22. Belknap and Carroll Counties were created. Belknap, with its seat at Laconia, was named for Jeremy Belknap, Pastor in Dover, New Hampshire and of the Federal Street Church in Boston, Massachusetts, founder of the Massachusetts Historical Society, who wrote the <u>History of New Hampshire</u> and other works.

Carroll, with its seat at Ossipee, was named for Charles Carroll, member of the Continental Congress, Senator from Maryland, and last surviving signer of the Declaration of Independence. |
| 1842 | Henry Hubbard, Democrat, became governor of New Hampshire and served in the office until 1844. |
| 1844 | John Hardy Steele, Democrat, became governor of the state and served in the office until 1846. |

CHRONOLOGY

1846	Anthony Colby, Democrat, became governor of the state and served in this capacity until 1847.
1847	Jared Warner Williams, Democrat, became governor of New Hampshire. He served in the office until 1849.
1849	Samuel Dinsmoor, Democrat, again became governor of the state and served in this capacity until 1852.
1850	Population: 317,976.
1852	August 3. Yale and Harvard held the first intercollegiate rowing race at Lake Winnepesaukee, New Hampshire. Harvard's crew won by four lengths.
	Noah Martin, Democrat, became governor of New Hampshire and served in the office until 1854.
	The state legislature abolished property qualifications for state offices.
1854	Nathaniel Bradley Baker, Democrat, became governor of the state and served in the office until 1855.
1855	Ralph Metcalf, American (Know-Nothing) Party, became governor of the state and served until 1857.
1857	William Haile, Republican, became governor of New Hampshire, and served in this capacity until 1859.
1859	Ichabod Goodwin, Republican became governor of the state and served in the office until 1861.
1860	Population: 326,073.
	Abraham Lincoln arrived in New Hampshire to deliver an address and to visit his son Robert who was attending Exeter Phillips Academy.
1861	Nathaniel Springer Berry, Republican, became governor of New Hampshire. He served in the office until 1863.

1863	Joseph Albree Gilmore, Republican, became governor of the state and served in the office until 1865.
1865	June 30. The state legislature ratified the 13th Amendment to the United States Constitution.
	Frederick Smyth, Unionist Republican, became governor of the state and served until 1867.
1866	July 7. The state legislature ratified the 14th Amendment to the United States Constitution.
	August 29. The residents of the state were asked to view the famous Mt. Washington Cog Railroad which had been built at Mt. Washington, New Hampshire. It was an invention of Sylvester Marsh. This was the first mountain-climbing railroad in the world and remained the steepest.
	The University of New Hampshire at Durham was founded as the New Hampshire College of Agriculture and Mechanic Arts at Hanover. The first classes met in 1868. The college moved to Durham in 1893 and adopted its present name in 1923.
1867	Walter Harriman, Republican, became governor of New Hampshire and served in the office until 1869.
1869	July 1. The state legislature ratified the 15th Amendment to the United States Constitution.
	Onslow Stearns, Republican, became governor of New Hampshire. He served in this capacity until 1871.
1870	Population: 318,300.
	Plymouth Normal School was established at Plymouth.
1871	James Adams Weston, Democrat, became governor of the state. He served in the office until 1872.
1872	Ezekiel Albert Straw, Republican, became governor of New Hampshire and served in the

office until 1874.

1874 James Adams Weston, Democrat, again became governor of the state and continued to serve in the office until 1875.

1875 Person Colby Cheney, Republican, became governor of the state in which capacity he served until 1877.

1877 Benjamin Franklin Prescott, Republican, became governor of New Hampshire, and served in the office until 1879.

1879 Natt Head, Republican, became governor of the state. He served in this capacity until 1881.

1880 Population: 346,991.

1881 Charles Henry Bell, Republican, became governor of the state and served in the office until 1883.

The first summer camp in the United States, intended for the use of city children, was established at Squam Lake.

1882 April 12. William E. Chandler was appointed Secretary of the Navy by President Chester A. Arthur. Chandler assumed his office as a member of the cabinet on April 17, 1882.

1883 Samuel Whitney Hale, Republican, became governor of the state and served in this capacity until 1885.

1885 Moody Currier, Republican, became governor of New Hampshire and served in the office until 1887.

1887 Charles Henry Sawyer, Republican, became governor of New Hampshire. He served in the office until 1889.

1889 David Harvey Goodell, Republican, became governor of the state. He served in this capacity until 1891.

1890 Population: 376,530.

1891 Hiram Americus Tuttle, Republican, became

	governor of the state. He served in the office until 1893.
1893	John Butler Smith, Republican, became governor of the state and served in this capacity until 1895.
	Saint Anselm's College was opened at Manchester.
1895	Charles Albert Busiel, Republican, became governor of New Hampshire and served in this capacity until 1897.
1897	George Allen Ramsdell, Republican, became governor of the state. He served in the office until January 3, 1899.
1899	January 5. Frank West Rollins, Republican, who had been elected in 1898, became governor of the state and served in the office until January 3, 1901.
1900	Population: 411,588.
1901	January 3. Chester Bradley Jordan, Republican, who had been elected governor in 1900, was inaugurated. He served in the gubernatorial office until January 1, 1903.
1903	January 1. Nahum Josiah Bachelder, Republican, who had been elected in 1902, became governor of New Hampshire. He served in this capacity until January 5, 1905.
	May 1. After 48 years of prohibition, the state legislature enacted a law providing licenses for liquor sales.
1905	January 5. John McLane, Republican, who had been elected in 1904, became governor of the state. He served until January 3, 1907.
1907	January 3. Charles M. Floyd, Republican, who had been elected governor of the state in 1906, was inaugurated. He served in the office until January 7, 1909.
1909	January 7. Henry B. Quinby, Republican, who had been elected in 1908, became governor of the state. He served in the office

until January 3, 1911.

The Keene Normal School was opened at Keene.

1910   Population: 430,572.

1911   January 5. Robert P. Bass, who had been elected in 1910, became governor of the state and served in the office until January 2, 1913

1913   January 2. Samuel D. Felker, Democrat, who had been elected in 1912, became governor of New Hampshire. He served in the office until January 7, 1915.

February 19. The state legislature ratified the 17th Amendment to the United States Constitution.

March 7. The state legislature ratified the 16th Amendment to the United States Constitution. It had originally rejected the Amendment on March 2, 1911.

1915   January 7. Rolland N. Spaulding, Republican, who had been elected governor of the state in 1914, was inaugurated. He served in the office until January 3, 1917.

1917   January 3. Henry W. Keyes, Republican, became governor of the state. He had been elected in 1916 and served in the office until January 2, 1919.

1919   January 2. John H. Bartlett, Republican, who had been elected in 1918, became governor of the state and served in the office until January 6, 1921.

January 15. The state legislature ratified the 18th Amendment to the United States Constitution.

1920   Population: 443,083.

1921   January 6. Albert O. Brown, who had been elected in 1920, became governor of New Hampshire. He served in the office until January 4, 1963.

1922	The state's first radio station, WLNH, began broadcasting at Laconia.
1923	January 4. Fred H. Brown, Democrat, who had been elected in 1922, became governor of the state. He served in the office until January 1, 1925.
1925	January 1. John G. Winant, Republican, became governor of New Hampshire. He had been elected in 1924 and served until January 6, 1927.
1927	January 6. Huntley N. Spaulding, Republican, who had been elected in 1926, became governor of the state. He served until the end of his term on January 3, 1929.
1929	January 3. Charles W. Tobey, Republican, who had been elected governor in 1928, was inaugurated. He served in the gubernatorial office until January 1, 1931.
1930	Population: 465,293.
1931	January 1. John G. Winant, Republican, who had been elected in 1930, became governor of the state. He was reelected in 1932, and served until January 3, 1935.
1933	January 31. The state legislature ratified the 20th Amendment to the United States Constitution.
	July 11. The state legislature ratified the 21st Amendment to the United States Constitution.
1935	January 3. H. Styles Bridges, Republican, who had been elected in 1934, became governor of the state. He served in the office until January 7, 1937.
1937	Francis P. Murphy, Republican, who had been elected in 1936, was inaugurated as governor of the state. He was reelected in 1938 and served in the office until January 2, 1941.
1940	Population: 491,524.
1941	January 2. Robert O. Blood, who had been elected in 1940, became governor of the

state. He was reelected in 1942 and served until January 4, 1945.

1944   The International Monetary Conference was held at Bretton Woods.

1945   January 4. Charles M. Dale, Republican, who had been elected in 1944, became governor of the state. He served until January 6, 1949.

1947   April 1. The state legislature ratified the 22nd Amendment to the United States Constitution.

1949   January 6. Sherman Adams, Republican, became governor of New Hampshire. He was reelected twice and served until January 1, 1953.

1950   Population: 533,242.

1953   January 1. Hugh Gregg, Republican, who had been elected in 1952, became governor of New Hampshire. He served in the office until January 6, 1955.

1954   The first television station in the state, WMUR-TV, began broadcasting from Manchester.

1955   January 6. Lane Dwinell, Republican, who had been elected in 1954, became governor of New Hampshire. He served in the office until January 1, 1959.

1959   **January 1.** Wesley Powell, Republican, became governor of the state. He had been elected in 1958 and served in the office until January 3, 1963.

1960   Population: 606,921.

1961   January 21. Luther H. Hodges became Secretary of Commerce in the Cabinet of President John F. Kennedy.

1961   March 30. The state legislature ratified the 23rd Amendment to the United States Constitution.

Alan B. Shepard, Jr. of East Denny became the first American to travel in space.

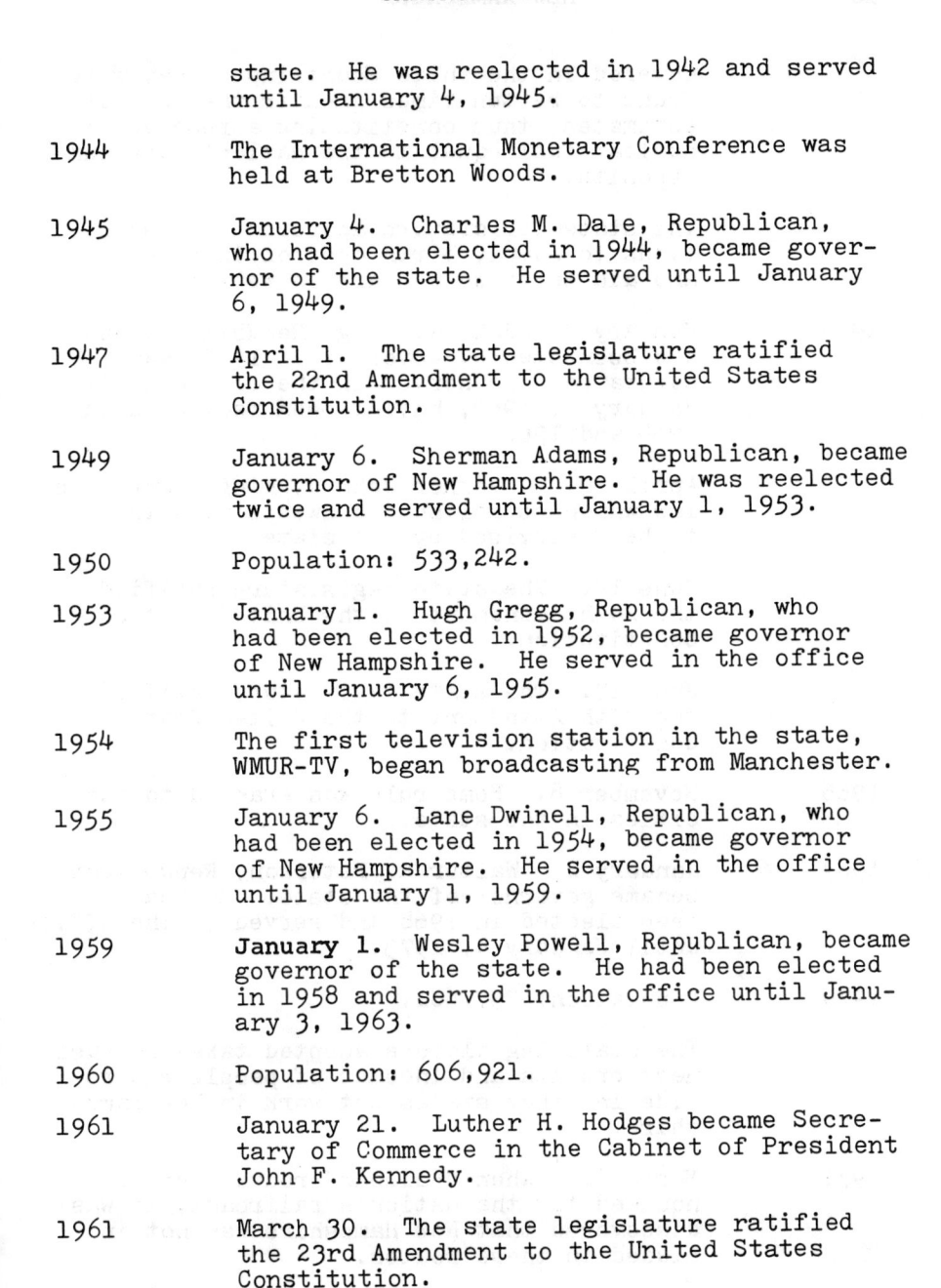

1962   December 2. Deposits of thorium were discovered in the White Mountains. They were found to be ten times greater than earlier estimates, thus constituting a reserve of nuclear fuel equal to the nation's uranium deposits.

The state legislature approved the use of funds to supply birth control information and aid to those who are on welfare.

1963   January 3. John W. King, Republican, who had been elected governor in 1962, was inaugurated. He served in the office until January 2, 1969, having been reelected in 1964 and 1966.

April 30. Governor John W. King signed the law which established a sweepstakes lottery to be supervised by the state.

June 12. The state legislature ratified the 24th Amendment to the United States Constitution.

June 13. The state legislature ratified the 25th Amendment to the United States Constitution.

1966   November 8. Home rule was granted to the cities in the state.

1969   January 2. Walter R. Peterson, Republican became governor of the state. He had been elected in 1968 and served in the office until January 4, 1973.

1970   Population: 737,681.

The state legislature adopted taxes on business profits and incomes of people who reside in other states but work in New Hampshire.

1971   March 22. When "Railpax" routes were announced for the nation's railroads, it was discovered that New Hampshire was not included in these routes.

May 13. The state legislature ratified the 26th Amendment to the United States Constitution.

1972   May 31. The Environmental Protection Agency

gave its approval for the state's clean air plans.

The state legislature ratified the Equal Rights Amendment to the United States Constitution.

1973

January 4. Meldrin Thomson, who had been elected in 1972, became governor of the state.

June 17. Douglas Castle, Administrator of the Environmental Protection Agency, said that the agency would approve the proposed water cooling system for the nuclear power plant at Seabrook.

July 26. The Atomic Safety and Licensing Board of the Nuclear Regulatory Commission ruled that proper safety precautions had been taken for the atomic energy plant planned for Seabrook, and that construction could begin on August 1.

1976

November 2. Governor Meldrim Thomson, Jr., Republican, was reelected.

December 13. The United States Supreme Court turned down a request by the state to review an Equal Opportunity Commission requirement that employers, including states, record and annually report the racial and ethnic identity of employees.

1977

April 30. Approximately 2,000 demonstrators marched on to a construction site of a nuclear power generating plant at Seabrook. The demonstrators refused to leave on May 1, whereupon 300 state police officers from New Hampshire and neighboring states began to arrest some of those present.

BIOGRAPHICAL DIRECTORY

The selected list of governors, United States Senators and Members of the House of Representatives for New Hampshire, 1789-1977, includes all persons listed in the Chronology for whom basic biographical data was readily available. Older biographical sources are frequently in conflict on certain individuals, and in such cases the source most commonly cited by later authorities was preferred.

BIOGRAPHICAL DIRECTORY

ADAMS, Sherman
    Republican
    d. East Dover, Vermont, January 8, 1899
    U. S. Representative, 1945-47
    Governor of New Hampshire, 1949-53

ATHERTON, Charles Gordon
    Democrat
    b. Amherst, N. H., July 4, 1804
    d. Manchester, Vermont, November 15, 1853
    U. S. Representative, 1837-43
    U. S. Senator, 1843-49

BADGER, William
    Democrat
    Governor of New Hampshire, 1834-36

BAKER, Henry Moore
    Republican
    b. Bow, near Concord, N. H., January 11, 1841
    d. Washington, D. C., May 30, 1912
    U. S. Representative, 1893-97

BAKER, Nathaniel B.
    Democrat
    Governor of New Hampshire, 1854-55

BARKER, David, Jr.
    ----
    b. Stratton, N. H., January 8, 1797
    d. Rochester, N. H., April 1, 1834
    U. S. Representative, 1827-29

BARTLETT, Ichabod
    Anti-Democrat
    b. Salisbury, N. H., July 24, 1786
    d. Portsmouth, N. H., October 19, 1853
    U. S. Representative, 1823-29

BARTLETT, John H.
    Republican
    b. Sunapee, N. H., March 15, 1869
    d. March 19, 1952
    Governor of New Hampshire, 1919-21

BARTLETT, Josiah
----
b. Amesbury, Mass., November 21, 1729
d. Kingston, N. H., May 19, 1795
President of New Hampshire, 1790-92
Governor of New Hampshire, 1792-94
    (Federalist)

BARTLETT, Josiah, Jr.
----
b. Kingston, N. H., August 29, 1768
d. Stratham, N. H., April 16, 1838
U. S. Representative, 1811-13

BASS, Perkins
Republican
b. East Walpole, Mass., October 6, 1912
U. S. Representative, 1955-63

BASS, Robert P.
Republican
b. Chicago, Ill., September 1, 1873
d. July 29, 1960
Governor of New Hampshire, 1911-13

BATCHELDER, Nahum J.
Republican
Governor of New Hampshire, 1903-05

BEAN, Benning Moulton
Democrat
b. Moultonboro, N. H., January 9, 1782
d. Moultonboro, N. H., February 6, 1866
U. S. Representative, 1833-37

BELL, Charles Henry
Republican
b. Chester, N. H., November 18, 1823
d. Exeter, N. H., November 11, 1893
U. S. Senator, 1879
Governor of New Hampshire, 1881-83

BELL, James
Whig
b. Francistown, N. H., November 13, 1804
d. Laconia, N. H., May 26, 1857
U. S. Senator, 1855-57

BELL, John
Adams Republican
Governor of New Hampshire, 1828-29

BELL, Samuel
    Jeffersonian Republican
    b. Londonderry, N. H., February 8, 1770
    d. Chester, N. H., December 23, 1850
    Governor of New Hampshire, 1819-23
    U. S. Senator, 1823-25

BELL, Samuel Newell
    Democrat
    b. Chester, N. H., March 25, 1829
    d. North Woodstock, N. H., February 8, 1889
    U. S. Representative, 1871-73, 1875-77

BENTON, Jacob
    Republican
    b. Waterford, Vermont, August 19, 1814
    d. Lancaster, N. H., September 29, 1892
    U. S. Representative, 1867-71

BERRY, Nathaniel S.
    Republican
    b. Bath, Maine, September 1, 1796
    d. Bristol, N. H., April 27, 1894
    Governor of New Hampshire, 1861-63

BETTON, Silas
    ----
    b. Londonderry, N. H., August 26, 1768
    d. Salem, N. H., January 22, 1822
    U. S. Representative, 1803-07

BLAIR, Henry William
    Republican
    b. Campton, N. H., December 6, 1834
    d. Washington, D. C., March 14, 1920
    U. S. Representative, 1875-79
    U. S. Senator, 1879-85, 1885-91
    U. S. Representative, 1893-95

BLAISDELL, Daniel
    Federalist
    b. Amesbury, Mass., January 22, 1762
    d. Canaan, N. H., January 10, 1833
    U. S. Representative, 1809-11

BLOOD, Robert O.
    Republican
    b. Enfield, N. H., November 10, 1887
    d. August, 1975
    Governor of New Hampshire, 1941-45

BRIDGES, Henry Styles
    Republican
    b. West Pembroke, Maine, September 9, 1898
    d. East Concord, N. H., November 26, 1961
    Governor of New Hampshire, 1934-36
    U. S. Senator, 1937-61

BRIGGS, James Frankland
    Republican
    b. Bury, Lancashire, England, October 23,
        1827
    d. Manchester, N. H., January 21, 1905
    U. S. Representative, 1877-83

BRODHEAD, John
    Democrat
    b. Lower Smithfield, Pa., October 5, 1770
    d. Newfields, N. H., April 7, 1838
    U. S. Representative, 1829-33

BROWN, Albert O.
    Republican
    b. Northwood, N. H., July 18, 1852
    d. March 28, 1937
    Governor of New Hampshire, 1921-23

BROWN, Fred Herbert
    Democrat
    b. Ossippe, N. H., April 12, 1879
    d. Somersworth, N. H., February 3, 1955
    Governor of New Hampshire, 1923-24
    U. S. Senator, 1933-39

BROWN, Titus
    ----
    b. Alstead, N. H., February 11, 1786
    d. Francestown, N. H., January 29, 1849
    U. S. Representative, 1825-29

BUFFUM, Joseph, Jr.
    Democrat
    b. Fitchburg, Mass., September 23, 1784
    d. Westmoreland, N. H., February 24, 1874
    U. S. Representative, 1819-21

BURKE, Edmund
    Democrat
    b. Westminster, Vermont, January 23, 1809
    d. Newport, N. H., January 25, 1882
    U. S. Representative, 1839-45

BURNHAM, Henry Eben
    Republican

b. Dumbarton, N. H., November 8, 1844
   d. Manchester, N. H., February 8, 1917
   U. S. Senator, 1901-13

BURNS, Robert
   Democrat
   b. Hudson, N. H., December 12, 1792
   d. Plymouth, N. H., June 26, 1866
   U. S. Representative, 1833-37

BURROUGHS, Sherman Everett
   Republican
   b. Dumbarton, N. H., February 6, 1870
   d. Washington, D. C., January 27, 1923
   U. S. Representative, 1917-23

BUSIEL, Charles A.
   Republican
   b. Meredith, N. H., ----
   d. 1901
   Governor of New Hampshire, 1895-97

BUTLER, Josiah
   Democrat
   b. Pelham, N. H., December 4, 1779
   d. Deerfield, N. H., October 27, 1854
   U. S. Representative, 1817-23

CARLETON, Peter
   Democrat
   b. Haverhill, Mass., September 19, 1755
   d. Landaff, N. H., April 29, 1828
   U. S. Representative, 1807-09

CHAMBERLAIN, John Curtis
   Federalist
   b. Worcester, Mass., June 5, 1772
   d. Utica, N. Y., December 8, 1834
   U. S. Representative, 1809-11

CHANDLER, Thomas
   Democrat
   b. Bedford, N. H., August 10, 1772
   d. Bedford, N. H., January 28, 1866
   U. S. Representative, 1829-33

CHANDLER, William Eaton
   Republican
   b. Concord, N. H., December 28, 1835
   d. Concord, N. H., November 20, 1917
   U. S. Secretary of the Navy, 1882-85
   U. S. Senator, 1887-89, 1889-1901

CHENEY, Person Colby
    Republican
    b. Holderness (now Ashland), N. H., February
        25, 1828
    d. Dover, N. H., June 19, 1901
    Governor of New Hampshire, 1875-77
    U. S. Senator, 1886-87

CILLEY, Bradbury
    Federalist
    b. Nottingham, N. H., February 1, 1760
    d. Nottingham, N. H., December 17, 1831
    U. S. Representative, 1813-17

CILLEY, Joseph
    Democrat
    b. Nottingham, N. H., January 4, 1791
    d. Nottingham, N. H., September 12, 1887
    U. S. Senator, 1846-47

CLAGETT, Clifton
    ----
    b. Portsmouth, N. H., December 3, 1762
    d. Amherst, N. H., January 25, 1829
    U. S. Representative, 1803-05, 1817-21

CLARK, Daniel
    Republican
    b. Stratham, N. H., October 24, 1809
    d. Manchester, N. H., January 2, 1891
    U. S. Senator, 1857-66, President pro
        tempore, 1864

CLARKE, Frank Gay
    Republican
    b. Wilton, N. H., September 10, 1850
    d. Peterboro, N. H., January 9, 1901
    U. S. Representative, 1897-1901

CLEVELAND, James Colgate
    Republican
    b. Montclair, N. J., June 13, 1920
    U. S. Representative, 1963-

COLBY, Anthony
    Whig
    Governor of New Hampshire, 1846-47

COTTON, Norris
    Republican
    b. Warren, N. H., May 11, 1900
    U. S. Representative, 1947-54
    U. S. Senator, 1954-

CRAGIN, Aaron Harrison
    American Party
    b. Weston, N. H., February 3, 1821
    d. Washington, D. C., May 10, 1898
    U. S. Representative, 1855-57 (American Party), 1857-59 (Republican)
    U. S. Senator, 1865-77 (American Party)

CURRY, Frank Dunklee
    Republican
    b. Canaan, N. H., October 30, 1853
    d. Canaan, N. H., November 25, 1921
    U. S. Representative, 1901-13

CURRIER, Moody
    Republican
    b. Boscawen, N. H., April 22, 1806
    d. Manchester, N. H., August 23, 1898
    Governor of New Hampshire, 1885-87

CUSHMAN, Samuel
    Democrat
    b. Portsmouth, N. H., June 8, 1783
    d. Portsmouth, N. H., May 20, 1851
    U. S. Representative, 1835-39

CUTTS, Charles
    Federalist
    b. Portsmouth, N. H., January 31, 1769
    d. Lewinsville, Va., January 25, 1846
    U. S. Senator, 1810-13, 1813

DALE, Charles M.
    Republican
    Governor of New Hampshire, 1945-49

DANIELL, Warren Fisher
    Democrat
    b. Newton Lower Falls, Mass., June 26, 1826
    d. Franklin, N. H., July 30, 1913
    U. S. Representative, 1891-93

DINSMOOR, Samuel, Sr.
    Jackson Democrat
    b. Windham, N. H., July 1, 1766
    d. Keene, N. H., March 15, 1835
    U. S. Representative, 1811-13
    Governor of New Hampshire, 1831-33

DINSMOOR, Samuel, Jr.
    Democrat
    Governor of New Hampshire, 1849-52

DREW, Irving Webster
　　Republican
　　b. Colebrook, N. H., January 8, 1845
　　d. Montclair, N. J., April 10, 1922
　　U. S. Senator, 1918

DURELL, Daniel Merve
　　----
　　b. Lee, N. H., July 20, 1769
　　d. Dover, N. H., April 29, 1841
　　U. S. Representative, 1807-09

DWINELL, Lane
　　Republican
　　b. Newport, Vermont, November 14, 1906
　　Governor of New Hampshire, 1955-59

EASTMAN, Ira Allen
　　Democrat
　　b. Gilmanton, N. H., January 1, 1809
　　d. Manchester, N. H., March 21, 1881
　　U. S. Representative, 1839-43

EASTMAN, Nehemiah
　　Democrat
　　b. Gilmanton, N. H., June 16, 1782
　　d. Farmington, N. H., January 11, 1856
　　U. S. Representative, 1825-27

EDWARDS, Thomas McKey
　　Republican
　　b. Keene, N. H., December 16, 1795
　　d. Keene, N. H., May 1, 1875
　　U. S. Representative, 1859-63

ELA, Jacob Hart
　　Republican
　　b. Rochester, N. H., July 18, 1820
　　d. Washington, D. C., August 21, 1884
　　U. S. Representative, 1867-71

ELLIS, Caleb
　　----
　　b. Walpole, Mass., April 16, 1797
　　d. Claremont, N. H., May 6, 1816
　　U. S. Representative, 1805-07

FARR, Evarts Worcester
　　Republican
　　b. Littleton, N. H., October 10, 1840
　　d. Littleton, N. H., November 30, 1880
　　U. S. Representative, 1879-80

FARRINGTON, James
    Democrat
    b. Conway, N. H., October 1, 1791
    d. Rochester, N. H., October 29, 1859
    U. S. Representative, 1837-39

FELKER, Samuel D.
    Democrat
    b. Rochester, N. H., April 16, 1859
    d. November 14, 1932
    Governor of New Hampshire, 1913-15

FLOYD, Charles M.
    Republican
    b. Derry, N. H., June 5, 1861
    d. 1923
    Governor of New Hampshire, 1907-09

FOGG, George Gilman
    Republican
    b. Meredith, N. H., May 26, 1813
    d. Concord, N. H., October 5, 1881
    U. S. Senator, 1866-67

FOSTER, Abiel
    ----
    b. Andover, Mass., August 8, 1735
    d. Canterbury, N. H., February 6, 1806
    Member Continental Congress, 1783-85
    U. S. Representative, 1789-91, 1795-1803

FREEMAN, Jonathan
    Federalist
    b. Mansfield, Conn., March 21, 1745
    d. Hanover, N. H., August 20, 1808
    U. S. Representative, 1797-1801

GALLINGER, Jacob Harold
    Republican
    b. Cornwall, Ontario, Canada, March 28, 1837
    d. Franklin, N. H., August 17, 1918
    U. S. Representative, 1885-89
    U. S. Senator, 1891-1918

GARDNER, Francis
    ----
    b. Leominster, Mass., December 27, 1771
    d. Roxbury, Mass., June 25, 1835
    U. S. Representative, 1807-09

GILMAN, John T.
    Federalist

b. Exeter, N. H., December 19, 1753
d. Portsmouth, N. H., August 31, 1828
Governor of New Hampshire, 1794-1805,
   1813-16

GILMAN, Nicholas
   Democrat
   b. Exeter, N. H., August 3, 1755
   d. Philadelphia, Pa., May 2, 1814
   Member Continental Congress, 1786-88
   U. S. Representative, 1789-97 (Federalist)
   U. S. Senator, 1805-14

GILMORE, Joseph A.
   Republican
   b. Weston, Vermont, June 10, 1811
   d. April 17, 1867
   Governor of New Hampshire, 1863-65

GOODELL, David H.
   Republican
   b. Hillsboro, N. H., May 6, 1834
   d. January 22, 1915
   Governor of New Hampshire, 1889-91

GOODWIN, Ichabod
   Republican
   b. North Berwick, Maine, October 8, 1794
   d. Portsmouth, N. H., July 4, 1882
   Governor of New Hampshire, 1859-61

GORDON, William
   ----
   b. near Boston, Mass., April 12, 1763
   d. Boston, Mass., May 8, 1802
   U. S. Representative, 1797-1800

GREGG, Hugh
   Republican
   b. Nashua, N. H., November 22, 1917
   Governor, 1953-55

HAILE, William
   Republican
   Governor of New Hampshire, 1857-59

HALE, Fletcher
   Republican
   b. Portland, Maine, January 22, 1883
   d. Brooklyn, N. Y., Naval Hospital,
      October 22, 1931
   U. S. Representative, 1925-31

HALE, John Parker
    Free-Soiler
    b. Rochester, N. H., March 31, 1806
    d. Dover, N. H., November 19, 1873
    U. S. Representative, 1843-45 (Democrat)
    U. S. Senator, 1847-53, 1855-65 (Free-
        Soiler)

HALE, Salma
    Democrat
    b. Alstead, N. H., March 7, 1787
    d. Somerville, Mass., November 19, 1866
    U. S. Representative, 1817-19

HALE, Samuel W.
    Republican
    Governor of New Hampshire, 1883-85

HALE, William
    Federalist
    b. Portsmouth, N. H., August 6, 1765
    d. November 8, 1848
    U. S. Representative, 1809-11, 1813-17

HALL, Joshua Gilman
    Republican
    b. Wakefield, N. H., November 5, 1828
    d. Stafford County, N. H., October 31,
        1898
    U. S. Representative, 1879-83

HALL, Obed
    Democrat
    b. Raynham, Mass., December 23, 1757
    d. Bartlett, N. H., April 1, 1828
    U. S. Representative, 1811-13

HAMMONS, Joseph
    Jackson Democrat
    b. Cornish, Maine, March 3, 1787
    d. Farmington, N. H., March 29, 1836
    U. S. Representative, 1829-33

HARPER, John Adams
    War Democrat
    b. Derryfield, N. H., November 2, 1779
    d. Meredith Bridge, N. H., June 18,
        1816
    U. S. Representative, 1811-13

HARPER, Joseph Morrill
    Democrat
    b. Limerick, Maine, June 21, 1787
    d. Canterbury, N. H., January 15, 1865
    Governor of New Hampshire, 1831
    U. S. Representative, 1831-35

HARRIMAN, Walter
　　Republican
　　b. Warner, N. H., April 8, 1817
　　d. Concord, N. H., July 25, 1884
　　Governor of New Hampshire, 1867-69

HARVEY, Jonathan
　　----
　　b. Sutton, N. H., February 25, 1780
　　d. North Sutton, N. H., August 23, 1859
　　U. S. Representative, 1825-31

HARVEY, Matthew
　　Democrat
　　b. Sutton, N. H., June 21, 1781
　　d. Concord, N. H., April 7, 1866
　　U. S. Representative, 1821-25
　　Governor of New Hampshire, 1830-31
　　U. S. District Court Judge, 1831-66

HAVEN, Nathaniel Appleton
　　Federalist
　　b. Portsmouth, N. H., July 19, 1762
　　d. Portsmouth, N. H., March 13, 1831
　　U. S. Representative, 1809-11

HAYNES, Martin Alonzo
　　Republican
　　b. Springfield, N. H., July 30, 1842
　　d. Lakeport, N. H., November 28, 1919
　　U. S. Representative, 1883-87

HEAD, Natt
　　Republican
　　Governor of New Hampshire, 1879-81

HEALY, Joseph
　　Democrat
　　b. Newton, Mass., August 21, 1776
　　d. Washington, N. H., October 10, 1861
　　U. S. Representative, 1825-29

HIBBARD, Ellery Albee
　　Democrat
　　b. St. Johnsbury, Vermont, July 31, 1826
　　d. Laconia, N. H., July 24, 1903
　　U. S. Representative, 1871-73

HIBBARD, Harry
　　Democrat
　　b. Concord, Vermont, June 1, 1816
　　d. Sommerville, Mass., July 28, 1872
　　U. S. Representative, 1849-55

HILL, Isaac
    Democrat
    b. West Cambridge, near Arlington, Mass.,
       April 6, 1788
    d. Washington, D. C., March 22, 1851
    U. S. Senator, 1831-36
    Governor of New Hampshire, 1836-39

HOLLIS, Henry French
    Democrat
    b. Concordia, N. H., August 30, 1869
    d. Paris, France, July 7, 1949
    U. S. Senator, 1913-19

HOUGH, David
    ----
    b. Norwich, Conn., March 13, 1753
    d. Lebanon, N. H., April 18, 1831
    U. S. Representative, 1803-07

HUBBARD, Henry
    Democrat
    b. Charlestown, N. H., May 3, 1784
    d. Charlestown, N. H., June 5, 1857
    U. S. Representative, 1829-35
    U. S. Senator, 1835-41
    Governor of New Hampshire, 1842-44

HUNT, Samuel
    ----
    b. Charlestown, D. H., July 8, 1765
    d. Gallipolis, Ohio, July 7, 1807
    U. S. Representative, 1802-05

HUOT, J. Oliva
    Democrat
    b. Laconia, N. H., August 11, 1917
    U. S. Representative, 1965-67

JOHNSON, James Hutchins
    ----
    b. Bath, N. H., June 3, 1802
    d. Bath, N. H., September 2, 1887
    U. S. Representative, 1845-49

JONES, Frank
    Democrat
    b. Barrington, N. H., September 15, 1832
    d. Portsmouth, N. H., October 2, 1902
    U. S. Representative, 1875-79

JORDAN, Chester B.
    Republican

b. Colebrook, N. H., October 15, 1837
d. August 24, 1914
Governor of New Hampshire, 1901-03

KEYES, Henry Wilder
  Republican
  b. Newbury, Vermont, May 23, 1863
  d. North Haverhill, N. H., June 19, 1938
  Governor of New Hampshire, 1917-19
  U. S. Senator, 1919-37

KING, John W.
  Democrat
  b. Manchester, N. H., October 10, 1918
  Governor of New Hampshire, 1963-69

KITTREDGE, George Washington
  Anti-Nebraska Democrat
  b. Epping, N. H., January 31, 1805
  d. Newmarket, N. H., March 6, 1881
  U. S. Representative, 1853-55

LANGDON, John
  Democrat
  b. Portsmouth, N. H., June 26, 1741
  d. Portsmouth, N. H., September 18, 1819
  Member Continental Congress, 1775-76, 1783
  President of New Hampshire, 1785-86, 1788-89
  U. S. Senator, 1789-1801, President pro tempore, 1789, 1792-94
  Governor of New Hampshire, 1805-09, 1810-12

LIVERMORE, Arthur
  Democrat
  b. Londonderry, N. H., July 29, 1766
  d. Campton, N. H., July 1, 1853
  U. S. Representative, 1817-21, 1823-25

LIVERMORE, Samuel
  ----
  b. Waltham, Mass., May 14, 1732
  d. Holderness, N. H., May 18, 1803
  Member Continental Congress, 1780-82, 1785
  U. S. Representative, 1789-93
  U. S. Senator, 1793-1801

MARCY, Daniel
  Democrat
  b. Portsmouth, N. H., November 7, 1809

d. Portsmouth, N. H., November 3, 1893
U. S. Representative, 1863-65

MARSTON, Gilman
    Republican
    b. Oxford, N. H., August 20, 1811
    d. Exeter, N. H., July 3, 1890
    U. S. Representative, 1859-63, 1865-67
    U. S. Senator, 1889

MARTIN, Noah
    Democrat
    Governor of New Hampshire, 1852-54

MASON, Jeremiah
    Federalist
    b. Lebanon, Conn., April 27, 1768
    d. Boston, Mass., October 14, 1848
    U. S. Senator, 1813-17

MATSON, Aaron
    ----
    b. Plymouth, Mass., 1770
    d. Newport, Vermont, July 18, 1855
    U. S. Representative, 1821-25

MCINTYRE, Thomas James
    Democrat
    b. Laconia, N. H., February 20, 1915
    U. S. Senator, 1962-

MCKINNEY, Luther Franklin
    Democrat
    b. Newport, Ohio, April 25, 1841
    d. Bridgton, Maine, July 30, 1922
    U. S. Representative, 1887-89, 1891-93

MCLANE, John
    Republican
    b. Lennoxtoun, Scotland, February 27,
        1852
    d. 1911
    Governor of New Hampshire, 1905-07

MERROW, Chester Earl
    Republican
    b. Center Ossippee, N. H., November 15,
        1906
    U. S. Representative, 1943-63

METCALF, Ralph
    American Party
    Governor of New Hampshire, 1855-57

MOORE, Orren Cheney
    Republican
    b. New Hampton, N. H., August 10, 1839
    d. Nashua, N. H., May 12, 1893
    U. S. Representative, 1889-91

MORRILL, David Lawrence
    Adams Democrat
    b. Epping, N. H., June 10, 1772
    d. Concord, N. H., January 28, 1849
    U. S. Senator, 1817-23
    Governor of New Hampshire, 1824-27

MORRISON, George Washington
    Democrat
    b. Fairlee, Vermont, October 16, 1809
    d, Manchester, N. H., December 21, 1888
    U. S. Representative, 1850-51, 1853-55

MOSES, George Higgins
    Republican
    b. Lubec, Maine, February 9, 1869
    d. Concord, N. H., December 20, 1944
    U. S. Senator, 1918-33, President pro
        tempore, 1925-33

MOULTON, Mace
    Democrat
    b. Concord, N. H., May 2, 1796
    d. Manchester, N. H., May 5, 1867
    U. S. Representative, 1845-47

MURPHY, Francis P.
    Republican
    b. Winchester, N. H., August 16, 1877
    d. December 19, 1958
    Governor of New Hampshire, 1937-41

MURPHY, Maurice J., Jr.
    Republican
    b. Dover, N. H., October 3, 1927
    U. S. Senator, 1961-62

NORRIS, Moses, Jr.
    Democrat
    b. Pittsfield, N. H., November 8, 1799
    d. Washington, D. C., January 11, 1855
    U. S. Representative, 1843-47
    U. S. Senator, 1849-55

NUTE, Alonzo
    Republican
    b. Milton, N. H., February 12, 1826

d. Farmington, N. H., December 24, 1892
U. S. Representative, 1889-91

OLCOTT, Simeon
    Federalist
    b. Bolton, Conn., October 1, 1735
    d. Charlestown, N. H., February 22, 1815
    U. S. Senator, 1801-05

PAGE, John
    Democrat
    b. Haverhill, N. H., May 21, 1787
    d. Haverhill, N. H., September 8, 1865
    U. S. Senator, 1836-37
    Governor of New Hampshire, 1839-42

PARKER. Hosea Washington
    Democrat
    b. Lempster, N. H., May 30, 1833
    d. Claremont, N. H., August 21, 1922
    U. S. Representative, 1871-75

PARKER, Nahum
    ----
    b. Shrewsbury, Mass., March 4, 1760
    d. Fitzwilliam, N. H., November 12, 1839
    U. S. Senator, 1807-10

PARROTT, John Faloyan
    Democrat
    b. Portsmouth, N. H., August 8, 1767
    d. Greenland, N. H., July 9, 1836
    U. S. Representative, 1817-19
    U. S. Senator, 1819-25

PATTERSON, James Willis
    Republican
    b. Henniker, N. H., July 2, 1823
    d. Hanover, N. H., July 2, 1823
    U. S. Representative, 1863-67
    U. S. Senator, 1867-73

PEASLEE, Charles Hazen
    Democrat
    b. Gilmanton, N. H., February 6, 1804
    d. St. Paul, Minn., September 18, 1866
    U. S. Representative, 1847-53

PEIRCE, Joseph
    ----
    b. Portsmouth, N. H., June 25, 1748
    d. Alton, N. H., September 12, 1812
    U. S. Representative, 1801-02

PERKINS, Jared
    Whig
    b. Unity, N. H., January 5, 1793
    d. Nashua, N. H., October 15, 1854
    U. S. Representative, 1851-53

PETERSON, Walter
    Republican
    b. Nashua, N. H., September 19, 1922
    Governor of New Hampshire, 1969-73

PICKERING, John
    ----
    b. Newington, N. H., September 22, 1737
    d. Portsmouth, N. H., April 11, 1805
    President of New Hampshire, 1789

PIERCE, Benjamin
    Jackson Republican
    b. Chelmford, Mass., December 25, 1757
    d. Hillsborough, N. H., April 1, 1839
    Governor of New Hampshire, 1827-28, 1829-30

PIERCE, Franklin
    Democrat
    b. Hillsboro, N. H., November 23, 1804
    d. Concord, N. H., October 8, 1869
    U. S. Representative, 1833-37
    U. S. Senator, 1837-42
    President of the United States, 1853-57

PIKE, Austin Franklin
    Republican
    b. Hebron, N. H., October 16, 1819
    d. Franklin, N. H., October 8, 1886
    U. S. Representative, 1873-75
    U. S. Senator, 1883-86

PIKE, James
    American Party
    b. Salisbury, Mass., November 10, 1818
    d. Newfields, N. H., July 26, 1895
    U. S. Representative, 1855-59

PLUMER, William
    Federalist
    b. Newburyport, Mass., June 25, 1759
    d. Epping, N. H., December 22, 1850
    U. S. Senator, 1802-07
    Governor of New Hampshire, 1812-13, 1816-19 (Democrat)

PLUMER, William, Jr.
    Democrat
    b. Epping, N. H., February 9, 1789
    d. Epping, N. H., September 18, 1854
    U. S. Representative, 1819-25

POWELL, Wesley
    Republican
    b. Portsmouth, N. H., October 13, 1915
    Governor of New Hampshire, 1959-63

PRESCOTT, Benjamin F.
    Republican
    Governor of New Hampshire, 1877-79

QUINBY, Henry B.
    Republican
    b. Biddeford, Maine, June 10, 1846
    d. February 8, 1924
    Governor of New Hampshire, 1909-11

RAMSDELL, George A.
    Republican
    Governor of New Hampshire, 1897-99

RAY, Ossian
    Republican
    b. Hinesburg, Vermont, December 13, 1835
    d. Lancaster, N. H., January 28, 1892
    U. S. Representative, 1881-85

REDING, John Randall
    Democrat
    b. Portsmouth, N. H., October 18, 1805
    d. Portsmouth, N. H., October 8, 1892
    U. S. Representative, 1841-45

REED, Eugene Elliott
    Democrat
    b. Manchester, N. H., April 23, 1866
    d. Manchester, N. H., December 15, 1940
    U. S. Representative, 1913-15

ROGERS, William Nathaniel
    Democrat
    b. Sanbornville, N. H., January 10, 1892
    d. Wolfeboro, N. H., September 25, 1945
    U. S. Representative, 1923-25, 1932-37

ROLLINS, Edward Henry
    Republican
    b. Somersworth (Rollinsford), N. H., Octo-

ber 3, 1824
    d. Isle of Shoals, N. H., July 3, 1889
    U. S. Representative, 1861-67
    U. S. Senator, 1877-83

ROLLINS, Frank W.
    Republican
    b. Concord, N. H., February 24, 1860
    d. October 27, 1915
    Governor of New Hampshire, 1899-1901

ROY, Alphonse
    Democrat
    b. St. Simon, Province of Quebec, Canada,
        October 26, 1897
    d. Manchester, N. H., October 5, 1967
    U. S. Representative, 1938-39

SAWYER, Charles H.
    Republican
    b. Watertown, N. Y., March 30, 1840
    d. 1908
    Governor of New Hampshire, 1887-89

SHAW, Tristram
    ----
    b. Hampton, N. H., May 23, 1786
    d. Exeter, N. H., March 14, 1843
    U. S. Representative, 1839-43

SHEAFE, James
    Federalist
    b. Portsmouth, N. H., November 16, 1755
    d. Portsmouth, N. H., December 5, 1829
    U. S. Representative, 1799-1801
    U. S. Senator, 1801-02

SHERBURNE, John Samuel
    ----
    b. Portsmouth, N. H., 1757
    d. Portsmouth, N. H., August 2, 1830
    U. S. Representative, 1793-97

SMALL, William Bradbury
    Republican
    b. Limington, Maine, May 17, 1817
    d. New Market, N. H., April 7, 1878
    U. S. Representative, 1873-75

SMITH, Jedediah Kilbum
    ----
    b. Amherst, N. H., November 7, 1770

    d. Amherst, N. H., December 17, 1828
    U. S. Representative, 1807-09

SMITH, Jeremiah
    Federalist
    b. Peterboro, N. H., November 29, 1759
    d. Dover, N. H., September 21, 1842
    U. S. Representative, 1791-97
    Governor of New Hampshire, 1809-10

SMITH, John D.
    Republican
    b. Saxton's River, Vermont, April 12, 1838
    d. August 10, 1914
    Governor of New Hampshire, 1893-95

SMITH, Samuel
    Federalist
    b. Peterboro, N. H., November 11, 1765
    d. Peterboro, N. H., April 25, 1842
    U. S. Representative, 1813-15

SMYTH, Frederick
    Unionist
    Governor of New Hampshire, 1865-67

SPAULDING, Huntley N.
    Republican
    b. Townsend Harbor, Mass., October 30, 1869
    d. November 14, 1955
    Governor of New Hampshire, 1927-29

SPAULDING, Rolland H.
    Republican
    b. Townsend Harbor, Mass., March 15, 1873
    d. March 14, 1942
    Governor of New Hampshire, 1915-17

SPRAGUE, Peleg
    ----
    b. Rochester, Mass., December 10, 1756
    d. Keene, N. H., April 20, 1800
    U. S. Representative, 1825-29
    U. S. Senator, 1829-35

STEARNS, Foster Waterman
    Republican
    b. Hull, Mass., July 29, 1881
    d. Exeter, N. H., June 4m 1956
    U. S. Representative, 1939-45

STEARNS, Onslow
    Republican

Governor of New Hampshire, 1869-71

STEELE, John H.
   Democrat
   Governor of New Hampshire, 1844-46

STEVENS, Aaron Fletcher
   Republican
   b. Londonderry, N. H., August 9, 1819
   d. Nashua, N. H., May 10, 1887
   U. S. Representative, 1867-71

STEVENS, Raymond Bartlett
   Democrat
   b. Binghamton, N. H., June 18, 1874
   d. Indianapolis, Ind., May 18, 1942
   U. S. Representative, 1913-15

STORER, Clement
   ----
   b. Kennebunk, Maine, September 20, 1760
   d. Portsmouth, N. H., November 21, 1830
   U. S. Representative, 1807-09
   U. S. Senator, 1817-19

STRAW, Ezekiel
   Republican
   Governor of New Hamphsire, 1872-74

SULLIVAN, George
   ----
   b. Durham, N. H., August 29, 1771
   d. Exeter, N. H., April 14, 1838
   U. S. Representative, 1811-13

SULLIVAN, John
   ----
   b. Somersworth, N. H., February 17, 1740
   d. Durham, N. H., January 23, 1795
   President of New Hampshire, 1786-88
   Governor of New Hampshire, 1789-90

SULLOWAY, Cyrus Adams
   Republican
   b. Grafton, N. H., June 8, 1839
   d. Washington, D. C., March 11, 1917
   U. S. Representative, 1895-1913, 1915-17

TAPPAN, Mason Weare
   Republican
   b. Newport, N. H., October 20, 1817
   d. Bradford, N. H., October 25, 1886
   U. S. Representative, 1855-61

TENNEY, Samuel
   b. Byefield, Mass., November 27, 1748
   d. Exeter, N. H., February 6, 1816
   U. S. Representative, 1800-07

THOMPSON, Meldrim, Jr.
   Republican
   Governor of New Hampshire, 1973-

THOMPSON, Thomas Weston
   b. Boston, Mass., March 15, 1766
   d. Concord. N. H., October 1, 1821
   U. S. Representative, 1805-07
   U. S. Senator, 1814-17

TOBEY, Charles William
   Republican
   b. Roxbury, Mass., July 22, 1880
   d. at the U. S. Naval Hospital at Bethesda,
      Md., July 24, 1953
   Governor of New Hampshire, 1929-31
   U. S. Representative, 1933-39
   U. S. Senator, 1939-53

TUCK, Amos
   Independent
   b. Parsonfield, N. H., August 2. 1810
   d. Exeter, N. H., December 11, 1879
   U. S. Representative, 1847-53

TUTTLE, Hiram A.
   Republican
   b. Barnstead, N. H., 1837
   d. 1911
   Governor of New Hampshire, 1891-93

UPHAM, George Baxter
   b. Brookfield, Mass., December 27, 1768
   d. Claremont, N. H., February 10, 1848
   U. S. Representative 1801-03

UPHAM, Nathaniel
   Democrat
   b. Deerfield, N. H., June 9, 1774
   d. Rochester, N. H., July 10, 1829
   U. S. Representative, 1817-23

UPTON, Robert William
   Republican
   b. Boston, Mass., February 3, 1884

U. S. Senator, 1953-54

VOSE, Roger
    Federalist
    b. Milton, Mass., February 24, 1763
    d. Walpole, N. H., October 26, 1841
    U. S. Representative, 1813-17

WADLEIGH, Bainbridge
    Republican
    b. Bradford, N. H., January 4, 1831
    d. Boston, Mass., January 24, 1891
    U. S. Senator, 1873-79

WASON, Edward Hills
    Republican
    b. New Boston, N. H., September 2, 1865
    d. on his estate near New Boston, N. H., February 6, 1941
    U. S. Representative, 1915-33

WEARE, Meshech
    ----
    b. Hampton Falls, N. H., January 16, 1713
    d. Hampton Falls, N. H., January 14, 1786
    President of New Hampshire, 1784-85

WEBSTER, Daniel
    Whig (New Hampshire/Massachusetts)
    b. Salisbury, (now Franklin), N. H., January 18, 1782
    d. Marshfield, Mass., October 24, 1852
    U. S. Representative, 1813-17 (Federalist - New Hampshire), 1823-27 (Federalist - Massachusetts)
    U. S. Senator, 1827-41 (Federalist), 1845-50 (Whig)
    U. S. Secretary of State, 1841-43, 1850-52

WEEKS, John Wingate
    ----
    b. Greenland, N. H., March 31, 1781
    d. Lancaster, N. H., April 3, 1853
    U. S. Representative, 1829-33

WEEKS, Joseph
    Democrat
    b. Warwick, Mass., February 13, 1773
    d. Winchester, N. H., August 4, 1845
    U. S. Representative, 1835-39

WELLS, John Sullivan
．．．．
    b. Durham, N. H., October 18, 1803
    d. Exeter, N.H., August 1, 1860
    U. S. Senator, 1855

WESTON, James A.
    Democrat
    Governor of New Hampshire, 1871-72, 1874-75

WHIPPLE, Thomas, Jr.
．．．．
    b. Lebanon, N. H., 1787
    d. Wentworth, N. H., January 23, 1835
    U. S. Representative, 1821-29

WILCOX, Jedathan
    Federalist
    b. Middletown, Conn., November 18, 1768
    d. Orford, N. H., July 18, 1839
    U. S. Representative, 1813-17

WILCOX, Leonard
    Democrat
    b. Hanover, N. H., January 29, 1799
    d. Orford, N. H., June 18, 1850
    U. S. Senator, 1842-43

WILLIAMS, Jared Warner
    Democrat
    b. West Woodstock, Conn., December 22, 1796
    d. Lancaster, N. H., September 29, 1864
    U. S. Representative, 1837-41
    Governor of New Hampshire, 1847-49
    U. S. Senator, 1853-54

WILSON, James
    Federalist
    b. Peterboro, N. H., August 16, 1766
    d. Keene, N. H., January 4, 1839
    U. S. Representative, 1809-11

WILSON, James (son of the preceding)
    Whig
    b. Peterboro, N. H., March 18, 1797
    d. Keene, N. H., May 29, 1881
    U. S. Representative, 1847-50

WINANT, John G.
    Republican
    b. New York, N. Y., February 23, 1889
    d. November 3, 1947

Governor of New Hampshire, 1925-27, 1931-35

WINGATE, Paine
Federalist
b. Amesbury, Mass., May 14, 1739
d. Stratham, N. H., March 7, 1838
Member Continental Congress, 1787-88
U. S. Senator, 1789-93
U. S. Representative, 1793-95

WOODBURY, Levi
Democrat
b. Francestown, N. H., December 22, 1789
d. Portsmouth, N. H., September 4, 1851
Governor of New Hampshire, 1823-24
U. S. Senator, 1825-31
U. S. Secretary of the Navy, 1831-34
U. S. Secretary of the Treasury, 1934-41
U. S. Senator, 1841-45
Associate Justice of the U. S. Supreme Court, 1845-51

WYMAN, Louis Crosby
Republican
b. Manchester, N. H., March 16, 1917
U. S. Representative, 1963-65, 1967-

PROMINENT PERSONALITIES

    The following select list of prominent persons of New Hampshire has been selected to indicate the valuable contributions they have made to American life.

PROMINENT PERSONALITIES

The following section lists of prominent personages of New Hampshire has been selected to indicate the valuable contributions they have made to American life.

PROMINENT PERSONALITIES

BLODGETT, Samuel
    b. Goffstown, N. H., August 28, 1757
    d. April 11, 1814
    Captain, New Hampshire Militia, 1775-77
    East India merchant
    Designed building for First Bank of the United States
    Engaged in lotteries in effort to promote development of District of Columbia - caused him financial ruin
    Imprisoned for debt

CHAMPHER, Benjamin
    b. New Ipswich, N. H., November 20, 1817
    d. 1907
    Began study of art in Boston, 1837
    Studied art in Paris, 1841-48
    Landscape and flower painter, painted White Mountain scenery and the wild flowers of New England
    Author: <u>Sixty Years; Memories of Art and Artists</u>, 1900

CHASE, Salmon Portland
    b. Cornish, N. H., January 13, 1808
    d. New York, N. Y., May 7, 1873
    U. S. Senator from Ohio, 1849-55, 1860
    Governor of Ohio, 1855-59
    U. S. Secretary of the Treasury, 1861-64
    Originated national banking system, 1863
    Chief Justice, U. S. Supreme Court, 1864-73

DANA, Charles A.
    b. Hinsdale, N. H., August 8, 1819
    d. October 17, 1897
    Member editorial staff, New York <u>Tribune</u>, 1847-62
    Assistant U. S. Secretary of War, 1863-64
    Coeditor, with George Ripley, <u>New American Cyclopaedia</u>, 16 vols., 1858-63
    Owner and editor, New York <u>Sun</u>, 1868-97

DOE, Charles
    b. Derry, N. H., April 4, 1830
    d. March 9, 1896
    Associate Justice New Hampshire Supreme Judicial Court, 1859-74
    Chief Justice, newly-formed, Supreme Court

of New Hampshire, 1876-96

EDDY, Mary Baker
    b. Bow, N. H., July 16, 1821
    d. 1910
    Discovered Christian Science, 1866
    Began teaching the "Science of Mind and
        Healing," 1867
    Founder of the Christian Science Church
    Chartered "Church of Christ, Scientist,"
        1879
    Author: *Church Manual*, 1895
    Founder, *The Christian Science Journal*, 1883
    Organizer, The Christian Science Publishing
        Society, 1898, publishers of *The Christian
        Science Quarterly*, *The Christian Science
        Monitor*, first published, 1908

EMERSON, Ralph Waldo
    b. Boston, Mass., May 25, 1803
    d. April 27, 1882
    Minister of Second Church of Boston, Unitarian, 1829-32
    Settled in Concord, Mass., 1834
    Published *Nature*, 1834 (contained basis of his transcendentalist philosophy)
    Published *Essays*, 1841, 1844 (2 vols.)

FROST, Robert L.
    b. San Francisco, March 26, 1874
    d. January 29, 1963
    Professor of English, Amherst, 1916-20, 1923-25, 1926-38
    Professor of Poetry, Harvard, from 1936
    Awarded Gold Medal, U. S. Senate, 1960
    Author: *A Boy's Will*, 1913
           New Hampshire, 1923
           A Witness Three, 1942
           The Gift Outright, 1961

GREELEY, Horace
    b. Amherst, N. H., February 3, 1811
    d. November 29, 1872
    Founded, with Jonas Winchester, the *New Yorker*, 1834
    Founded New York *Tribune*, 1841, merged *New Yorker* into the *Tribune*
    Democratic candidate for President of the United States, 1872

HADDOCK, Charles B.
    b. Salisbury, N. H., June 20, 1796
    d. January 15, 1861

First Professor of Rhetoric and Oratory,
    Dartmouth, 1819-38
Professor of Intellectual Philosophy and
    Political Economy, 1838-40
Member, New Hampshire House of Representa-
    tives, 1845-48
Chargé d'Affaires to Portugal, 1850-54

HALE, Sarah Josepha Buell
    b. Newport, N. H., October 24, 1788
    d. April 30, 1879
    Editor, Ladies Magazine, Boston, 1828-37
    Editor, Godey's Lady's Book, 1837-77
    Author: Northwood, 1827
        Poems for Our Children, 1830 (con-
        tained "Mary's Lamb")

STARK, John
    b. Londonderry, N. H., August 28, 1728
    d. Manchester, N. H., May 2, 1822
    Fought in French and Indian War
    Colonel at Battle of Bunker Hill, 1775
    Brigadier General, Continental Army

STONE, Harlan F.
    b. Chesterfield, N. H., October 11, 1872
    d. April 22, 1946
    Professor of Law, Columbia Law School,
        1902-05
    Dean, Columbia Law School, 1910-23
    U. S. Attorney General, 1924-25
    Associate Justice, U. S. Supreme Court,
        1925-41
    Chief Justice U. S. Supreme Court, 1941-
        46

SULLIVAN, John
    b. Somersworth, N. H., February 17, 1740
    d. Durham, N. H., January 23, 1795
    Member, Continental Congress, 1774, 1775,
        1780, 1781
    Led unsuccessful attack against British
        on Staten Island, August, 1777
    Commanded American forces besieging New-
        port, 1778
    Led Sullivan-Clinton expedition, defeated
        combined Indian-Loyalist contingent
        near Elmira, N. Y., August, 1779
    Attorney General of New Hampshire, 1782-
        86
    President of New Hampshire, 1786, 1787,
        1789
    U. S. District Judge of N. H., 1789-95

NEW HAMPSHIRE

THAXTER, Celia L.
    b. Portsmouth, N. H., June 29, 1835
    d. Appledore, Island, off New Hampshire,
        August 26, 1894
    Author of following works of poetry:
        <u>Poems</u>, 1872
        <u>Driftweed</u>, 1879
        <u>Poems for Children</u>, 1884
        <u>Idyls and Pastorals</u>, 1886
        <u>An Island Garden,</u> 1894

TUCK, Amos
    b. Parsonfield, Maine, August 2, 1810
    d. Exeter, N. H., December 11, 1879
    U. S. Representative, 1847-53
    Trustee of Dartmouth, 1857-66
    Amos Tuck School of Administration and Finance, Dartmouth, established, 1900, in his honor

WENTWORTH, Benning
    b. Portsmouth, N. H., July 24, 1696
    d. Little Harbor, N. H., October 14, 1770
    First royal governor of New Hampshire, 1741-67
    Made extensive land grants, known as New Hampshire grants, in area west and east of Connecticut River, claimed by both New York and New Hampshire, causing disputes between two colonies, settled by creation of Vermont

WENTWORTH, John
    b. Portsmouth, N. H., August 20, 1737
    d. Halifax, Nova Scotia, April 8, 1820
    Succeeded his uncle Benning Wentworth as governor of New Hampshire, 1767
    Loyalist at outbreak of American Revolution, forced to flee
    Lieutenant Governor of Nova Scotia, 1792-1808
    Created Baronet, 1795

FIRST STATE CONSTITUTION

Constitution of 1776

In Congress at Exeter, January 5, 1776.

VOTED, That this Congress take up CIVIL GOVERNMENT for this colony in manner and form following, viz.

WE, the members of the Congress of New Hampshire, chosen and appointed by the free suffrages of the people of said colony, and authorized and empowered by them to meet together, and use such means and pursue such measures as we should judge best for the public good; and in particular to establish some form of government, provided that measure should be recommended by the Continental Congress: And a recommendation to that purpose having been transmitted to us from the said Congress: Have taken into our serious consideration the unhappy circumstances, into which this colony is involved by means of many grievous and oppressive acts of the British Parliament, depriving us of our natural and constitutional rights and privileges; to enforce obedience to which acts a powerful fleet and army have been sent to this country by the ministry of Great Britain, who have exercised a wanton and cruel abuse of their power, in destroying the lives and properties of the colonists in many places with fire and sword, taking the ships and lading from many of the honest and industrious inhabitants of this colony employed in commerce, agreeable to the laws and customs a long time used here.

The sudden and abrupt departure of his Excellency John Wentworth, Esq., our late Governor, and several of the Council, leaving us destitute of legislation, and no executive courts being open to punish criminal offenders; whereby the lives and properties of the honest people of this colony are liable to the machinations and evil designs of wicked men, *Therefore*, for the preservation of peace and good order, and for the security of the lives and properties of the inhabitants of this colony, we conceive ourselves reduced to the necessity of establishing A FORM OF GOVERNMENT to continue during the present unhappy and unnatural contest with Great Britain; PROTESTING and DECLARING that we neaver sought to throw off our dependance upon Great Britain, but felt ourselves happy under her protection, while we could enjoy our constitutional rights and privileges. And that we shall rejoice if such a reconciliation between us and our parent State can be effected as shall be approved by the CONTINENTAL CONGRESS, in whose prudence and wisdom we confide.

Accordingly pursuant to the trust reposed in us, WE DO RESOLVE, that this Congress assume the name, power and authority of a house of Representatives or Assembly for the *Colony of New-Hampshire*. And that said House then proceed to choose twelve persons, being reputable freeholders and inhabitants within this colony, in the following manner, viz. five in the county of Rockingham, two in the county of Strafford, two in the county of Hillsborough, two in the county of Cheshire, and one in the county of Grafton, to be a distinct and separate branch of the Legislature by the name of a COUNCIL for this colony, to continue as such until the third Wednesday in December next; any seven of whom to be a quorum to do business. That such Council appoint their President, and in his absence that the senior counsellor preside; that a Secretary be appointed by both branches, who may be a counssellor, or otherwise, as they shall choose.

That no act or resolve shall be valid and put into execution unless agreed to, and passed by both branches of the legislature.

That all public officers for the said colony, and each county, for the current year, be appointed by the Council and Assembly, except the several clerks of the Executive Courts, who shall be appointed by the Justices of the respective Courts.

That all bills, resolves, or votes for raising, levying and collecting money originate in the house of Representatives.

That at any session of the Council and Assembly neither branch shall adjourn from any longer time than from Saturday till the next Monday without consent of the other.

And it is further resolved, That if the present unhappy dispute with Great Britain should continue longer than this present year, and the Continental Congress give no instruction or direction to the contrary, the Council be chosen by the people of each respective county in such manner as the Council and house of Representatives shall order.

That general and field officers of the militia, on any vacancy, be appointed by the two houses, and all inferior officers be chosen by the respective companies.

That all officers of the Army be appointed by the two houses, except they should direct otherwise in case of any emergency.

That all civil officers for the colony and for each county be appointed, and the time of their continuance in office be determined by the two houses, except clerks of Courts, and county treasurers, and recorders of deeds.

That a treasurer, and a recorder of deeds for each county be annually chosen by the people of each county respectively; the votes for such officers to be returned to the respective courts of General Sessions of the Peace in the county, there to be ascertained as the Council and Assembly shall hereafter direct.

That precepts in the name of the Council and Assembly, signed by the President of the Council, and Speaker of the house of Representatives, shall issue annually at or before the first day of November, for the choice of a Council and house of Representatives to be returned by the third Wednesday in December then next ensuing, in such manner as the Council and Assembly shall hereafter prescribe.

Constitution of 1784

PART I.—THE BILL OF RIGHTS.

ARTICLE I.

All men are born equally free and independent; therefore, all government of right originates from the people, is founded in consent, and instituted for the general good.

II. All men have certain natural, essential, and inherent rights; among which are—the enjoying and defending life and liberty—acquiring, possessing and protecting property—and in a word, of seeking and obtaining happiness.

III. When men enter into a state of society, they surrender up some of their natural rights to that society, in order to insure the protection of others; and, without such an equivalent, the surrender is void.

IV. Among the natural rights, some are in their very nature unalienable, because no equivalent can be given or received for them. Of this kind are the RIGHTS OF CONSCIENCE.

V. Every individual has a natural and unalienable right to worship GOD according to the dictates of his own conscience, and reason; and no subject shall be hurt, molested, or restrained in his person, liberty or estate for worshipping GOD, in the manner and season most agreeable to the dictates of his own conscience, or for his religious profession, sentiments or persuasion; provided he doth not disturb the public peace, or disturb others, in their religious worship.

VI. As morality and piety, rightly grounded on evangelical principles, will give the best and greatest security to government, and will lay in the hearts of men the strongest obligations to due subjection; and as the knowledge of these, is most likely to be propagated through a society by the institution of the public worship of the DEITY, and of public instruction in morality and religion; therefore, to promote those important purposes, the people of this state have a right to impower, and do hereby fully impower the legislature to authorize from time to time, the several towns, parishes, bodies-corporate, or religious societies within this state, to make adequate provision at their own expence, for the support and maintenance of public protestant teachers of piety, religion and morality:

Provided notwithstanding, That the several towns, parishes, bodies-corporate, or religious societies, shall at all times have the exclusive right of electing their own public teachers, and of contracting with them for their support and maintenance. And no person of any one particular religious sect or denomination, shall ever be compelled to pay towards the support of the teacher or teachers of another persuasion, sect or denomination.

And every denomination of christians demeaning themselves quietly, and as good subjects of the state, shall be equally under the protection of the law: and no subordination of any one sect or denomination to another, shall ever be established by law.

And nothing herein shall be understood to affect any former contracts made for the support of the ministry; but all such contracts shall remain, and be in the same state as if this constitution had not been made.

VII. The people of this state, have the sole and exclusive right of governing themselves as a free, sovereign, and independent state, and do, and forever hereafter shall, exercise and enjoy every power, jurisdiction and right pertaining thereto, which is not, or may not hereafter be by them expressly delegated to the United States of America in Congress assembled.

VIII. All power residing originally in, and being derived from the people, all the magistrates and officers of government, are their substitutes and agents, and at all times accountable to them.

IX. No office or place whatsoever in government, shall be hereditary—the abilities and integrity requisite in all, not being transmissible to posterity or relations.

X. Government being instituted for the common benefit, protection, and security of the whole community, and not for the private interest or emolument of any one man, family or class of men; therefore, whenever the ends of government are perverted, and public liberty manifestly endangered, and all other means of redress are ineffectual, the people may, and of right ought, to reform the old, or establish a new government. The doctrine of non-resistance against arbitrary power, and oppression, is absurd, slavish, and destructive of the good and happiness of mankind.

XI. All elections ought to be free, and every inhabitant of the state having the proper qualifications, has equal right to elect, and be elected into office.

XII. Every member of the community has a right to be protected by it in the enjoyment of his life, liberty and property; he is therefore bound to contribute his share in the expence of such protection, and to yield his personal service when necessary, or an equivalent. But no part of a man's property shall be taken from him, or applied to public uses, without his own consent, or that of the representative body of the people. Nor are the inhabitants of this state controllable by any other laws than those to which they or their representative body have given their consent.

XIII. No person who is conscientiously scrupulous about the lawfulness of bearing arms, shall be compelled thereto, provided he will pay on equivalent.

XIV. Every subject of this state is entitled to a certain remedy, by having recourse to the laws, for all injuries he may receive in his person, property or character, to obtain right and justice freely, without being obliged to purchase it; completely, and without any denial; promptly, and without delay, conformably to the laws.

XV. No subject shall be held to answer for any crime, or offence, until the same is fully and plainly, substantially and formally, described to him; or be compelled to accuse or furnish evidence against himself. And every subject shall have a right to produce all proofs that may be favorable to himself; to meet the witnesses against him face to face, and to be fully heard in his defence by himself, and counsel. And no subject shall be arrested, imprisoned, despoiled, or deprived of his property, immunities, or privileges, put out of the protection of the law, exiled or deprived of his life, liberty, or estate, but by the judgment of his peers or the law of the land.

XVI. No subject shall be liable to be tried, after an acquittal, for the same crime or offence.—Nor shall the legislature make any law that shall subject any person to a capital punishment, excepting for the government of the army and navy, and the militia in actual service, without trial by jury.

XVII. In criminal prosecutions, the trial of facts in the vicinity where they happen, is so essential to the security of the life, liberty and estate of the citizen, that no crime or offence ought to be tried in any other county than that in which it is committed; except in cases of general insurrection in any particular county, when it shall appear to the Judges of the Superior Court, that an impartial trial cannot be had in the county where the offence may be committed, and upon their report, the assembly shall think proper to direct the trial in the nearest county in which an impartial trial can be obtained.

XVIII. All penalties ought to be proportioned to the nature of the offence. No wise legislature will affix the same punishment to the crimes of theft, forgery and the like, which they do to those of murder and treason; where the same undistinguishing severity is exerted against all offences; the people are led to forget the real distinction in the crimes themselves, and to commit the most flagrant with as little compunction as they do those of the lightest dye: For the same reason a multitude of sanguinary laws is both impolitic and unjust. The true design of all punishments being to reform, not to exterminate, mankind.

XIX. Every subject hath a right to be secure from all unreasonable searches and seizures of his person, his houses, his papers, and all his possessions. All warrants, therefore, are contrary to this right, if the cause or foundation of them be not previously supported by oath, or affirmation; and if the order in the warrant to a civil officer, to make search in suspected places, or to arrest one or more suspected persons, or to seize their property, be not accompanied with a special designation of the persons or objects of search, arrest, or seizure; and no warrant ought to be issued but in cases, and with the formalities prescribed by the laws.

XX. In all controversies concerning property, and in all suits between two or more persons, except in cases in which it has been heretofore otherwise used and practiced, the parties have a right to a trial by jury; and this method of procedure shall be held sacred, unless in causes arising on the high seas, and such as relate to mariners wages, the legislature shall think it necessary hereafter to alter it.

XXI. In order to reap the fullest advantage of the inestimable privilege of the trial by jury, great care ought to be taken that none but qualified persons should be appointed to serve; and such ought to be fully compensated for their travel, time and attendance.

XXII. The Liberty of the Press is essential to the security of freedom in a state; it ought, therefore, to be inviolably preserved.

XXIII. Retrospective laws are highly injurious, oppressive and unjust. No such laws, therefore, should be made, either for the decision of civil causes, or the punishment of offences.

XXIV. A well regulated militia is the proper, natural, and sure defence of a state.

XXV. Standing armies are dangerous to liberty, and ought not to be raised or kept up without the consent of the legislature.

XXVI. In all cases, and at all times, the military ought to be under strict subordination to, and governed by the civil power.

XXVII. No soldier in time of peace, shall be quartered in any house without the consent of the owner; and in time of war, such quarters ought not to be made but by the civil magistrate, in a manner ordained by the legislature.

XXVIII. No subsidy, charge, tax, impost or duty shall be established, fixed, laid, or levied, under any pretext whatsover, without the consent of the people or their representatives in the legislature, or authority derived from that body.

XXIX. The power of suspending the laws, or the execution of them, ought never to be exercised but by the legislature, or by authority derived therefrom, to be exercised in such particular cases only as the legislature shall expressly provide for.

XXX. The freedom of deliberation, speech, and debate, in either house of the legislature, is so essential to the rights of the people, that it cannot be the foundation of any action, complaint, or prosecution, in any other court or place whatsoever.

XXXI. The legislature ought frequently to assemble for the redress of grievances, for correcting, strengthening and confirming the laws, and for making new ones, as the common good may require.

XXXII. The people have a right in an orderly and peaceable manner, to assemble and consult upon the common good, give instructions to their representatives; and to request of the legislative body, by way of petition or remonstrance, redress of the wrongs done them, and of the grievances they suffer.

XXXIII. No magistrate or court of law shall demand excessive bail or sureties, impose excessive fines, or inflict cruel or unusual punishments.

XXXIV. No person can in any case be subjected to law martial, or to any pains, or penalties, by virtue of that law, except those employed in the army or navy, and except the militia in actual service, but by authority of the legislature.

XXXV. It is essential to the preservation of the rights of every individual, his life, liberty, property and character, that there be an impartial interpretation of the laws, and administration of justice. It is the right of every citizen to be tried by judges as impartial as the lot of humanity will admit. It is therefore not only the best policy, but for the security of the rights of the people, that the judges of the supreme (or superior) judicial court should hold their offices so long as they behave well; and that they should have honorable salaries, ascertained and established by standing laws.

XXXVI. Economy being a most essential virtue in all states, especially in a young one; no pension shall be granted, but in consideration of actual services, and such pensions ought to be granted with great caution, by the legislature, and never for more than one year at a time.

XXXVII. In the government of this state, the three essential powers thereof, to wit, the legislative, executive and judicial, ought to be kept as separate from and independent of each other, as the nature of a free government will admit, or as is consistent with that chain of connection that binds the whole fabric of the constitution in one indissoluble bond of union and amity.

XXXVIII. A frequent recurrence to the fundamental principles of the Constitution, and a constant adherence to justice, moderation, temperance, industry, frugality, and all the social virtues, are indispensably necessary to preserve the blessings of liberty and good government; the people ought, therefore, to have a particular regard to all those principles in the choice of their officers and representatives: and they have a right to require of their law-givers and magistrates, an exact and constant observance of them in the formation and execution of the laws necessary for the good administration of government.

PART II.—THE FORM OF GOVERNMENT.

THE people inhabiting the territory formerly called the Province of New-Hampshire, do hereby solemnly and mutually agree with each other, to form themselves into a free, sovereign, and independent Body-politic, or State, by the name of the STATE OF NEW HAMPSHIRE.

THE GENERAL COURT

THE supreme legislative power within this state shall be vested in the senate and house of representatives, each of which shall have a negative on the other.

THE senate and house shall assemble every year on the first Wednesday of June, and at such other times as they may judge necessary; and shall dissolve, and be dissolved, seven days next preceding the said first Wednesday of June; and shall be stiled THE GENERAL COURT OF NEW-HAMPSHIRE.

THE general court shall forever have full power and authority to erect and constitute judicatories and courts of record, or other courts, to be holden in the name of the state, for the hearing, trying, and determining all manner of crimes, offences, pleas, processes, plaints, actions, causes, matters and things whatsover, arising, or happening within this state, or between or concerning persons inhabiting or residing, or brought within the same, whether the same be criminal or civil, or whether the crimes be capital or not capital, and whether the said pleas be real, personal, or mixed; and for the awarding and issuing execution thereon. To which courts and judicatories are hereby given and granted full power and authority, from time to time to administer oaths or affirmations, for the better discovery of truth in any matter in controversy, or depending before them.

AND farther, full power and authority are hereby given and granted to the said general court, from time to time, to make, ordain and establish, all manner of wholesome and reasonable orders, laws, statutes, ordinances, directions and instructions, either with penalties or without; so as the same be not repugnant, or contrary to this constitution, as they may judge for the benefit and welfare of this state, and for the governing and ordering thereof, and of the subjects of the same, for the necessary support and defence of the government thereof; and to frame and settle annually, or provide by fixed laws, for the naming and settling all civil officers within this state; such officers excepted, the election and appointment of whom, are hereafter in this form of government otherwise provided for; and to set forth the several duties, powers and limits, of the several civil and military officers of this state, and the forms of such oaths or affirmations, as shall be respectively administered unto them for the execution of their several offices and places, so as the same be not repugnant or contrary to this constitution; and also to impose fines, mulcts, imprisonments, and other punishments; and to impose and levy proportional and reasonable assessments, rates and taxes, upon all the inhabitants of, and residents within the said state; and upon all estates within the same; to be issued and disposed of by warrant under the hand of the president of this state for the time being, with the advice and consent of the council, for the public service, in the necessary defence and support of the government of this state, and the protection and preservation of the subjects thereof, according to such acts as are, or shall be in force within the same.

AND while the public charges of government or any part thereof, shall be assessed on polls and estates in the manner that has heretofore been practiced; in order that such assessments may be made with equality, there shall be a valuation of the estates within the state taken anew once in every five years at least, and as much oftener as the general court shall order.

SENATE.

THERE shall be annually elected by the freeholders and other inhabitants of this state, qualified as in this constitution is provided, twelve persons to be senators for the year ensuing their election; to be chosen in and by the inhabitants of the districts, into which this state may from time to time be divided by the general court, for that purpose: and the general court in assigning the number to be elected by the respective districts, shall govern themselves by the proportion of public taxes paid by the said districts; and timely make known to the inhabitants of the state, the limits of each district, and the number of senators to be elected therein; provided the number of such districts shall never be more than ten, nor less than five.

AND the several counties in this state, shall, until the general court shall order otherwise, be districts for the election of senators, and shall elect the following number, viz.

ROCKINGHAM, five. STRAFFORD, two. HILLSBOROUGH, two. CHESHIRE, two. GRAFTON, one.

THE senate shall be the first branch of the legislature: and the senators shall be chosen in the following manner, viz. Every male inhabitant of each town and parish with town privileges in the several counties in this state, of twenty-one years of age and upwards, paying for himself a poll tax, shall have a right at the annual or other meetings of the inhabitants of said towns and parishes, to be duly warned and holden annually forever in the month of March; to vote in the town or parish wherein he dwells, for the senators in the county or district whereof he is a member.

AND every person qualified as the constitution provides, shall be considered an inhabitant for the purpose of electing and being elected into any office or place within this state, in that town, parish and plantation where he dwelleth and hath his home.

THE selectmen of the several towns and parishes aforesaid, shall, during the choice of senators, preside at such meetings impartially, and shall receive the votes of all the inhabitants of such towns and parishes present and qualified to vote for senators, and shall sort and count the same in the meeting, and in presence of the town-clerk, who shall make a fair record in presence of the selectmen, and in open meeting, of the name of every person voted for, and the number of votes against his name; and a fair copy of this record shall be attested by the selectmen and town-clerk, and shall be sealed up and directed to the secretary of the state, with a superscription expressing the purport thereof, and delivered by said clerk to the sheriff of the county in which such town or parish lies, thirty days at least, before the first Wednesday of June; and the sheriff of each county, or his deputy, shall deliver all such certificates by him received, into the secretary's office, seventeen days at least, before the first Wednesday of June.

AND the inhabitants of plantations and places unincorporated, qualified as this constitution provides, who are or shall be required to assess taxes upon themselves towards the support of government, or shall be taxed therefor, shall have the same privilege of voting for senators in the plantations and places wherein they reside, as the inhabitants of the respective towns and parishes aforesaid have. And the meetings of such plantations and places for that purpose, shall be holden annually in the month of March, at such places respectively therein, as the assessors thereof shall direct; which assessors shall have like authority for notifying the electors, collecting and returning the votes, as the selectmen and town-clerks have in their several towns by this constitution.

AND, that there may be a due meeting of senators, on the first Wednesday of June, annually, the president and three of the council for the time being, shall as soon as may, examine the returned copies of such records; and fourteen days before the said first Wednesday of June, he shall issue his summons to such persons as appear to be chosen senators by a majority of votes, to attend and take their seats on that day: *Provided, nevertheless,* that for the first year the said returned copies shall be examined by the president and five of the council of the former constitution of government; and the said president shall in like manner notify the persons elected, to attend and take their seats accordingly.

THE senate shall be final judges of the elections, returns, and qualifications of their own members, as pointed out in this constitution, and shall on the said first Wednesday of June annually, determine and declare, who are elected by each district to be senators by a majority of votes: and in case there shall not appear to be the full number returned elected by a majority of votes for any district, the deficiency shall be supplied in the following manner, viz. The members of the house of representatives and such senators as shall be declared elected, shall take the names of such persons as shall be found to have the highest number of votes in each district, and not elected, amounting to twice the number of senators wanting, if there be so many voted for; and out of these shall elect by joint ballot the number of senators wanted for such district: and in this manner all such vacancies shall be filled up in every district of the state, and in like manner all vacancies in the senate, arising by death, removal out of the state, or otherwise, shall be supplied as soon as may be after such vacancies happen.

Provided nevertheless, 'That no person shall be capable of being elected a senator, who is not of the protestant religion, and seized of a freehold estate in his own right of the value of *two hundred pounds,* lying within this state, who is not of the age of thirty years, and who shall not have been an inhabitant of this state for seven years immediately preceding his election; and at the time thereof he shall be an inhabitant of the district for which he shall be chosen.

THE senate shall have power to adjourn themselves, provided such adjournment do not exceed two days at a time.

THE senate shall appoint their own officers, and determine their own rules of proceedings. And not less than seven members of the senate shall make a quorum for doing business; and when less than eight senators shall be present, the assent of five at least shall be necessary to render their acts and proceedings valid.

The senate shall be a court with full power and authority to hear and determine all impeachments made by the house of representatives, against any officer or officers of the state, for misconduct or mal-administration in their offices. But previous to the trial of any such impeachment, the members of the senate shall respectively be sworn, truly and impartially to try and determine the charge in question according to evidence. Their judgment, however, shall not extend farther than removal from office, disqualification to hold or enjoy any place of honor, trust or profit under this state; but the party so convicted, shall nevertheless be liable to indictment, trial, judgment, and punishment, according to laws of the land.

HOUSE OF REPRESENTATIVES.

THERE shall be in the legislature of this state a representation of the people annually elected and founded upon principles of equality: and in order that such representation may be as equal as circumstances will admit, every town, parish or place intitled to town privileges, having one hundred and fifty rateable male polls, of twenty-one years of age, and upwards, may elect one representative; if four hundred and fifty rateable polls, may elect two representatives; and so proceeding in that proportion, making three hundred such rateable polls the mean increasing number, for every additional representative.

Such towns, parishes or places as have less than one hundred and fifty rateable polls shall be classed by the general-assembly for the purpose of chusing a representative, and seasonably notified thereof. And in every class formed for the above-mentioned purpose, the first annual meeting shall be held in the town, parish, or place wherein most of the rateable polls reside; and afterwards in that which has the next-highest number, and so on annually by rotation, through the several towns, parishes or places, forming the district.

WHENEVER any town, parish, or place intitled to town privileges as aforesaid, shall not have one hundred and fifty rateable polls, and be so situated as to render the classing thereof with any other town, parish, or place very inconvenient, the general-assembly may upon application of a majority of the voters in such town, parish, or place, issue a writ for their electing and sending a representative to the general-court.

THE members of the house of representatives shall be chosen annually in the month of March, and shall be the second branch of the legislature.

ALL persons qualified to vote in the election of senators shall be intitled to vote within the town, district, parish, or place where they dwell, in the choice of representatives. Every member of the house of representatives shall be chosen by ballot; and for two years at least next preceding his election, shall have been an inhabitant of this state, shall have an estate within the town, parish, or place which he may be chosen to represent, of the value of *one hundred pounds,* one half of which to be a freehold, whereof he is seized in his own right; shall be at the time of his election, an inhabitant of the town, parish, or place he may be chosen to represent; shall be of the protestant religion, and shall cease to represent such town, parish, or place immediately on his ceasing to be qualified as aforesaid.

THE travel of each representative to the general-assembly, and returning home, once in every session, and no more, shall be at the expence of the state, and the wages for his attendance, at the expence of the town, parish, or places he represents; such members attending seasonably, and not departing without licence. All intermediate vacancies in the house of representatives, may be filled up from time to time, in the same manner as annual elections are made.

THE house of representatives shall be the grand inquest of the state, and all impeachments made by them, shall be heard and tried by the senate.

ALL money bills shall originate in the house of representatives, but the senate may propose or concur with amendments as on other bills.

THE house of representatives shall have power to adjourn themselves, but no longer than two days at a time.

A majority of the members of the house of representatives shall be a quorum for doing business; but when less than two-thirds of the representatives elected shall be present, the assent of two-thirds of those members shall be necessary to render their acts and proceedings valid.

No member of the house of representatives or senate, shall be arrested or held to bail on mean process, during his going to, returning from, or attendance upon the court.

THE house of representatives shall choose their own speaker, appoint their own officers, and settle the rules of proceedings in their own house. They shall have authority to punish by imprisonment, every person who shall be guilty of disrespect to the house in its presence, by any disorderly or contemptuous behaviour, or by threatening, or ill treating any of its members; or by obstructing its deliberations; every person guilty of a breach of its privileges in making arrests for debt, or by assaulting any member during his attendance at any session; in assaulting or disturbing any one of its officers in the execution of any order or procedure of the house, in assaulting any witness, or other person, ordered to attend by and during his attendance of the house, or in rescuing any person arrested by order of the house, knowing them to be such. The senate, president and council, shall have the same powers in like cases; provided that no imprisonment by either, for any offence, exceed ten days.

THE journals of the proceedings of both houses of the general-court, shall be printed and published, immediately after every adjournment, or prorogation; and upon motion made by any one member, the yeas and nays upon any question, shall be taken and entered in the journals.

EXECUTIVE POWER.—PRESIDENT.

THERE shall be a supreme executive magistrate, who shall be stiled, THE PRESIDENT OF THE STATE OF NEW-HAMPSHIRE; and whose title shall be HIS EXCELLENCY.

THE PRESIDENT shall be chosen annually; and no person shall be eligible to this office, unless at the time of his election, he shall have been an inhabitant of this state for seven years next preceding, and unless he shall be of the age of thirty years; and unless he shall, at the same time, have an estate of the value of *five hundred pounds*, one half of which shall consist of a freehold, in his own right, within the state; and unless he shall be of the protestant religion.

THOSE persons qualified to vote for senators and representatives, shall within the several towns, parishes or places, where they dwell, at a meeting to be called for that purpose, some day in the month of March annually, give in their votes for a president to the selectmen, who shall preside at such meeting, and the clerk in the presence and with the assistance of the selectmen, shall in open meeting sort and count the votes, and form a list of the persons voted for, with the number of votes for each person against his name, and shall make a fair record of the same in the town books, and a public declaration thereof in the said meeting; and shall in the presence of said inhabitants, seal up a copy of said list attested by him and the selectmen, and transmit the same to the sheriff of the county, thirty days at least before the first Wednesday of June, or shall cause returns of the same to be made to the office of the secretary of the state, seventeen days at least, before said day, who shall lay the same before the senate and house of representatives on the first Wednesday of June, to be by them examined: and in case of an election by a majority of votes through the state, the choice shall be by them declared, and published; but if no person shall have a majority of votes, the house of representatives shall by ballot elect two out of the four persons who had the highest number of votes, if so many shall have been voted for; but if otherwise, out of the number voted for; and make return to the senate of the two persons so elected, on which the senate shall proceed by ballot to elect one of them who shall be declared president.

THE president of the state shall preside in the senate, shall have a vote equal with any other member; and shall also have a casting vote in case of a tie.

THE president with advice of council, shall have full power and authority in the recess of the general court, to prorogue the same from time to time, not exceeding ninety days in any one recess of said court; and during the session of said court, to adjourn or prorogue it to any time the two houses may desire, and to call it together sooner than the time to which it may be adjourned, or prorogued, if the welfare of the state should require the same.

IN cases of disagreement between the two houses, with regard to the time of adjournment, or prorogation, the president, with advice of council, shall have a right to adjourn or prorogue the general court, not exceeding ninety days, at any one time, as he may determine the public good may require. And he shall dissolve the same seven days before the said first Wednesday of June. And in case of any infectious distemper prevailing in the place where the said court at any time is to convene, or any other cause whereby dangers may arise to the healths or lives of the members from their attendance, the president may direct the session to be holden at some other the most convenient place within the State.

THE president of this state for the time being, shall be commander in chief of the army and navy, and all the military forces of the state, by sea and land; and shall have full power by himself, or by any chief commander, or other officer, or officers, from time to time, to train, instruct, exercise and govern the militia and navy; and for the special defence and safety of this state to assemble in martial array, and put in warlike posture, the inhabitants thereof, and to lead and conduct them, and with them to encounter, expulse, repel, resist and pursue by force of arms, as well by sea as by land, within and without the limits of this state; and also to kill slay, destroy, if necessary, and conquer by all fitting ways, enterprize and means, all and every such person and persons as shall, at any time hereafter, in a hostile manner, attempt or enterprize the destruction, invasion, detriment, or annoyance of this state; and to use and exercise over the army and navy, and over the militia in actual service, the law-martial in time of war, invasion, and also in rebellion, declared by the legislature to exist, as occasion shall necessarily require: and surprize by all ways and means whatsoever, all and every such person or persons, with their ships, arms, ammunition, and other goods, as shall in a hostile manner invade or attempt the invading, conquering, or annoying this state: and in fine, the president hereby is entrusted with all other powers incident to the office of captain-general and commander in chief, and admiral, to be exercised agreeably to the rules and regulations of the constitution, and the laws of the land; provided that the president shall not at any time hereafter, by virtue of any power by this constitution granted, or hereafter to be granted to him by the legislature, transport any of the inhabitants of this state, or oblige them to march out of the limits of the same, without their free and voluntary consent, or the consent of the general court, nor grant commissions for exercising the law-martial in any case, without the advice and consent of the council.

THE power of pardoning offences, except such as persons may be convicted of before the senate by impeachment of the house, shall be in the president by and with the advice of the council: but no charter of pardon granted by the president with advice of council, before conviction, shall avail the party pleading the same, notwithstanding any general or particular expressions contained therein, descriptive of the offence or offences intended to be pardoned.

ALL judicial officers, the attorney-general, solicitor-general, all sheriffs, coroners, registers of probate, and all officers of the navy, and general and field-officers of the militia, shall be nominated and appointed by the president and council; and every such nomination shall be made at least seven days prior to such appointment, and no appointment shall take place, unless three of the council agree thereto. The captains and subalterns in the respective regiments shall be nominated and recommended by the field-officers to the president, who is to issue their commissions immediately on receipt of such recommendation.

No officer duly commissioned to command in the militia, shall be removed from his office, but by the address of both houses to the president, or by fair trial in court-martial, pursuant to the laws of the state for the time being.

THE commanding officers of the regiments shall appoint their adjutants and quarter-masters; the brigadiers their brigade-majors, the major-generals their aids; the captains,and subalterns their non-commissioned officers.

THE president and council, shall appoint all officers of the continental army, whom by the confederation of the United States it is provided that this state shall appoint, as also all officers of forts and garrisons.

THE division of the militia into brigades, regiments and companies, made in pursuance of the militia laws now in force, shall be considered as the proper division of the militia of this state, until the same shall be altered by some future law.

No monies shall be issued out of the treasury of this state, and disposed of (except such sums as may be appropriated for the redemption of bills of credit or treasurer's notes, or for the payment of interest arising thereon) but by warrant under the hand of the president for the time being, by and with the advice and consent of the council, for the necessary support and defence of this state, and for the necessary protection and preservation of the inhabitants thereof, agreeably to the acts and resolves of the general court.

ALL public boards, the commissary-general, all superintending officers of public magazines and stores, belonging to this state, and all commanding officers of forts and garrisons within the same, shall once in every three months, officially, and without requisition, and at other times, when required by the president, deliver to him an account of all goods, stores, provisions, ammunition, cannon, with their appendages, and small arms, with their accoutrements, and of all other public property under their care respectively; distinguishing the quantity, and kind of each, as particularly as may be; together with the condition of such forts and garrisons: and the commanding officer shall exhibit to the president, when required by him, true and exact plans of such forts, and of the land and sea, or harbour or harbours adjacent.

THE president and council shall be compensated for their services from time to time by such grants as the general court shall think reasonable.

PERMANENT and honorable salaries shall be established by law for the justices of the superior court.

WHENEVER the chair of the president shall be vacant, by reason of his death, absence from the state, or otherwise, the senior senator for the time being, shall, during such vacancy, have and exercise all the powers and authorities which by this constitution the president is vested with when personally present.

COUNCIL.

ANNUALLY, on the first meeting of the general court, two members of the senate and three from the house of representatives, shall be chosen by joint ballot of both houses as a council, for advising the president in the executive part of government, whom the president for the time being, shall have full power and authority to convene from time to time, at his discretion, and the president with the counsellors, or three of them at least, shall and may from time to time hold and keep a council, for ordering and directing the affairs of the state according to the laws of the land.

THE qualifications for counsellors, shall be the same as those required for senators. The members of the council shall not intermeddle with the making or trying impeachments, but shall themselves be impeachable by the house, and triable by the senate for mal-conduct.

THE resolutions and advice of the council shall be recorded in a register, and signed by the members present, and this record may be called for at any time, by either house of the legislature, and any member of the council may enter his opinion contrary to the resolution of the majority.

AND whereas the elections appointed to be made by this constitution on the first Wednesday of June annually, by the two houses of the legislature, may not be completed on that day, the said elections may be adjourned from day to day until the same shall be completed. And the order of the elections shall be as follows: the vacancies in the senate, if any, shall be first filled up; the president shall then be elected, provided there should be no choice of him by the people: and afterwards the two houses shall proceed to the election of the council.

SECRETARY, TREASURER, COMMISSARY-GENERAL, &c.

THE Secretary, treasurer, and commissary-general, shall be chosen by joint ballot of the senators and representatives assembled in one room.

THE records of the state shall be kept in the office of the secretary, who may appoint his deputies, for whose conduct he shall be answerable, and he shall attend the president and council, the senate and representatives, in person or by deputy, as they may require.

COUNTY-TREASURER, &c.

THE County-treasurers, and registers of deeds shall be elected by the inhabitants of the several towns, in the several counties in the state, according to the method now practiced, and the present laws of the state: and before they enter upon the business of their offices, shall be respectively sworn faithfully to discharge the duties thereof, and shall severally give bond with sufficient sureties, in a reasonable sum for the use of the county, for the punctual performance of their respective trusts.

JUDICIARY POWER.

THE tenure, that all commission officers shall have by law in their offices, shall be expressed in their respective commissions. All judicial officers, duly appointed, commissioned and sworn, shall hold their offices during good behaviour, excepting those concerning whom there is a different provision made in this constitution: *Provided nevertheless*, the president, with consent of council, may remove them upon the address of both houses of the legislature.

EACH branch of the legislature, as well as the president and council, shall have authority to require the opinions of the justices of the superior court upon important questions of law, and upon solemn occasions.

IN order that the people may not suffer from the long continuance in place of any justice of the peace, who shall fail in discharging the important duties of his office with ability and fidelity, all commissions of justices of the peace shall become void, at the expiration of five years from their respective dates; and upon the expiration of any commission, the same may, if necessary, be renewed, or another person appointed, as shall most conduce to the well-being of the state.

THE judges of probate of wills, and for granting letters of administration, shall hold their courts at such place or places, on such fixed days, as the convenience of the people may require. And the legislature shall, from time to time, hereafter appoint such times and places, until which appointments, the said courts shall be holden at the times and places which the respective judges shall direct.

ALL causes of marriage, divorce and alimony, and all appeals from the respective judges of probate, shall be heard and tried by the superior court, until the legislature shall, by law make other provision.

CLERKS OF COURTS.

THE clerks of the superior court of judicature, inferior courts of common pleas, and general sessions of the peace, shall be appointed by the respective courts during pleasure. And to prevent any fraud or unfairness in the entries and records of said courts, no such clerk shall be of counsel in any cause in the court of which he is clerk, nor shall he fill any writ in any civil action whatsoever.

DELEGATES TO CONGRESS.

THE delegates of this state to the Congress of the United States, shall some time between the first Wednesday of June, and the first Wednesday of September annually, be elected by the senate and house of representatives in their separate branches; to serve in Congress for one year, to commence on the first Monday in November then next ensuing. They shall have commissions under the hand of the president, and the great seal of the state; but may be recalled at any time within the year, and others chosen and commissioned, in the same manner, in their stead: and they shall have the same qualifications, in all respects, as by this constitution are required for the president.

No person shall be capable of being a delegate to Congress, for more than three years in any term of five years; nor shall any person being a delegate, be capable of holding any office under the United States, for which he, or any other for his benefit, receives any salary, or emolument of any kind.

ENCOURAGEMENT OF LITERATURE, &c.

KNOWLEDGE, and learning, generally diffused through a community, being essential to the preservation of a free government; and spreading the opportunities and advantages of education through the various parts of the country, being highly conducive to promote this end; it shall be the duty of the legislators and the magistrates, in all future periods of this government to cherish the interest of literature and the sciences, and all seminaries and public schools, to encourage private and public institutions, rewards and immunities for the promotion of agriculture, arts, sciences, commerce, trades, manufactures and natural history of the country; to countenance and inculcate the principles of humanity and general benevolence, public and private charity, industry and economy, honesty and punctuality, sincerity, sobriety, and all social affections, and generous sentiments, among the people.

OATH and subscriptions; exclusion from offices; commissions; writs; confirmation of laws; habeas corpus; the enacting stile; continuance of officers; provision for a future revision of the constitution, &c.

ANY person chosen president, counsellor, senator, or representative, military or civil officer, (town officers excepted,) accepting the trust, shall, before he proceeds to execute the duties of his office, make and subscribe the following declaration, viz.

I, A. B. do truly and sincerely acknowledge, profess, testify and declare, that the state of New-Hampshire is, and of right ought to be, a free, sovereign and independent state; and do swear that I will bear faith and true allegiance to the same, and that I will endeavor to defend it against all treacherous conspiracies and hostile attempts whatever: and I do further testify and declare, that no man or body of men, hath or can have, a right to absolve me from the obligation of this oath, declaration or affirmation; and that I do make this acknowledgement, profession, testimony, and declaration, honestly and truly, according to the common acceptation of the foregoing words, without any equivocation, mental evasion or secret reservation whatever.

So help me GOD.

I, A. B. do solemnly and sincerely swear and affirm, that I will faithfully and impartially discharge and perform all the duties incumbent on me as according to the best of my abilities, agreeably to the rules and regulations of this constitution, and the laws of the state of New-Hampshire. So help me GOD.

Provided always, When any person chosen or appointed as aforesaid, shall be of the denomination called quakers, or shall be scrupulous of swearing, and shall decline taking the said oaths, such shall take and subscribe them omitting the word *"swear,"* and likewise the words *"So help me God,"* subjoined instead thereof, *This I do under the pains and penalties of perjury.*

AND the oaths or affirmations shall be taken and subscribed by the president before the senior senator present, in the presence of the two houses of assembly; and by the senate and representatives first elected under this constitution, before the president and council for the time being; and by the residue of the officers aforesaid, before such persons, and in such manner as from time to time shall be prescribed by the legislature.

ALL commissions shall be in the name of the state of New Hampshire, signed by the president, and attested by the secretary, or his deputy, and shall have the great seal of the state affixed thereto.

ALL writs issuing out of the clerk's office in any of the courts of law, shall be in the name of the state of New-Hampshire; shall be under the seal of the court whence they issue, and bear test of the chief, first, or senior justice of the court; but when such justice shall be interested, then the writ shall bear test of some other justice of the court, to which the same shall be returnable; and be signed by the clerk of such court.

ALL indictments, presentments and informations shall conclude against the peace and dignity of the state.

THE estates of such persons as may destroy their own lives, shall not for that offence be forfeited, but descend or ascend in the same manner, as if such persons had died in a natural way. Nor shall any article which shall accidentally occasion the death of any person, be henceforth deemed a deodand, or in any wise forfeited on account of such misfortune.

ALL the laws which have heretofore been adopted, used and approved, in the province, colony, or state of New-Hampshire, and usually practiced on in the courts of law, shall remain and be in full force, until altered and repealed by the legislature; such parts thereof only excepted, as are repugnant to the rights and liberties contained in this constitution: Provided that nothing herein contained, when compared with the twenty-third article in the bill of rights, shall be construed to affect the laws already made respecting the persons or estates of absentees.

THE privilege and benefit of the habeas corpus, shall be enjoyed in this state, in the most free, easy, cheap, expeditious, and ample manner, and shall not be suspended by the legislature, except upon the most urgent and pressing occasions, and for a time not exceeding three months.

THE enacting stile in making and passing acts, statutes and laws, shall be—*Be it enacted by the senate and house of representatives, in general court convened.*

No president or judge of the superior court, shall hold any office or place under the authority of this state, except such as by this constitution they are admitted to hold, saving that the judges of the said court may hold the offices of justices of the peace throughout the state; nor shall they hold any place or office, or receive any pension or salary, from any other state, government, or power whatever.

No person shall be capable of exercising at the same time, more than one of the following offices within this state, viz. Judge of probate, sheriff, register of deeds; and never more than two offices of profit, which may be held by appointment of the president, or president and council, or senate and house of representatives, or superior or inferior courts; military offices, and offices of justices of the peace, excepted.

No person holding the office of judge of the superior court, secretary, treasurer of the state, judge of probate, attorney-general, commissary-general, judge of the maritime court, or judge of the court of admiralty, military officers receiving pay from the continent or this state, excepting officers of the militia occasionally called forth on an emergency; judge of the inferior court of common pleas, register of deeds, president, professor or instructor of any college, sheriff, or office of the customs, including naval-officers, shall at the same time have a seat in the senate or house of representatives, or council; but their being chosen or appointed to, and accepting the same, shall operate as a resignation of their seat in the senate, or house of representatives, or council; and the place so vacated shall be filled up.

No person shall ever be admitted to hold a seat in the legislature, or any office of trust or importance under this government, who in the due course of law, has been convicted of bribery or corruption, in obtaining an election or appointment.

In all cases where sums of money are mentioned in this constitution, the value thereof shall be computed in silver, at *six shillings and eight pence* per ounce.

To the end that there may be no failure of justice or danger arise to this state from a change in the form of government, all civil and military officers, holding commissions under the government and people of New-Hampshire, and other officers of the said government and people, at the time this constitution shall take effect, shall hold, exercise and enjoy all the powers and authorities to them granted and committed, until other persons shall be appointed in their stead. All courts of law in the business of their respective departments, and the executive, and legislative bodies and persons, shall continue in full force, enjoyment and exercise of all their trusts and employments, until the general court, and the supreme and other executive officers under this constitution, are designated, and invested with their respective trusts, powers and authority.

This form of government shall be enrolled on parchment, and deposited in the secretary's office, and be a part of the laws of the land, and printed copies thereof shall be prefixed to the books containing the laws of this state, in all future editions thereof.

To preserve an effectual adherence to the principles of the constitution, and to correct any violations thereof, as well as to make such alterations therein, as from experience may be found necessary, the general court shall at the expiration of seven years from the time this constitution shall take effect, issue precepts, or direct them to be issued from the secretary's office, to the several towns and incorporated places, to elect delegates to meet in convention for the purposes aforesaid: the said delegates to be chosen in the same manner, and proportioned as the representatives to the general assembly; provided that no alteration shall be made in this constitution before the same shall be laid before the towns and unincorporated places, and approved by two-thirds of the qualified voters present, and voting upon the question.

IN CONVENTION, HELD AT CONCORD, THE THIRTY-FIRST DAY OF OCTOBER, 1783.

THE Returns from the several towns being examined, and it appearing that the foregoing BILL OF RIGHTS AND FORM OF GOVERNMENT, were approved of by the PEOPLE; the same are hereby agreed on and established by the DELEGATES OF THE PEOPLE, and declared to be the CIVIL CONSTITUTION FOR THE STATE OF NEW-HAMPSHIRE, to take place on the first Wednesday of June, 1784; and that in the mean time the General Court under the present government, make all the necessary arrangements for introducing this Constitution, at that time, and in the manner therein described.

NATHANIEL FOLSOM, President, P. T.

J. M. SEWALL, Secretary.

SELECTED DOCUMENTS

    The documents selected for this section have been chosen to reflect the interests or attitudes of the contemporary observer or writer. Documents relating specifically to the constitutional development of New Hampshire will be found in volume six of <u>Sources and Documents of United States Constitutions</u>, a companion reference collection to the Columbia University volumes previously cited.

SELECTED DOCUMENTS

THE CONDITION OF NEW HAMPSHIRE -- 1730/1

The following report to the Lords of Trade and Plantations indicates many aspects of life in the colony including trade, natural resources, the conditions of the population, and the government.

Source: Albert Bushnell Hart, ed. *American History Told By Contemporaries*. Vol. II. New York: The Macmillan Company, 1898.

The Condition of New Hampshire (1730/1)
BY LIEUTENANT-GOVERNOR JOHN WENTWORTH

This piece, very similar in character to those in Nos. 19 above and 22 below, is unsigned, but appears to be by Wentworth, who was at this date the only representative of the home government. — Bibliography: Winsor, *Narrative and Critical History*, V, 163-164; Channing and Hart, *Guide*, § 123. — For previous New Hampshire history, see *Contemporaries*, I, ch. xix.

*A*NSWERS *to the Queries sent from the Right Honorable the Lords of Trade and Plantations.* — *January* 22, 1730.

1. The situation of the province of New-Hampshire, is between the province of the Massachusetts Bay, and the late province of Maine, bordering about fifteen miles in width upon the Atlantic Sea, or Western Ocean. — The nature of the country, as to the ground, is rough, uneven, and hilly, but for the most part a good soil, being a mixture of clay land and loam, well watered, and suitably adapted for hemp and flax, and having considerable meadows in it. As to the climate, 'tis cold. Portsmouth, the capital of the province, is in forty three degrees and twenty minutes north latitude, and sixty eight degrees west from London, settled by good observations.

2. The province has no other boundaries than what are expressed in the King's commission to the Governor, and they are from three miles to the northward of Merrimack river on the one side, to Pascataqua river on the other, and no other bounds are mentioned in the said commission, and both of them are in dispute with the government of the Massachusetts Bay.

3. As to the Constitution of the government, the supreme power here, is vested in the Governor and Council, (appointed by the King,) and a house of representatives, (chosen by the people,) who make laws, &c.

4. The trade of the province is lumber and fish. The number of shipping belonging to the province, are five, consisting of about five hundred tons; and there are about three or four hundred tons of other shipping, that trade here (annually) not belonging to the province. The seafaring men, are about forty. The trade is much the same as it hath been, for some years past.

5. The province makes use of all sorts of British manufactures amounting to about five thousand pounds sterling, annually in value, which are had principally from Boston.

6. The trade of this province to other plantations is to the Caribbee Islands, whither we send lumber and fish, and receive for it rum, sugar, molasses and cotton; and as to the trade from hence to Europe, it is to Spain, or Portugal, from whence our vessels bring home salt.

7. The method to prevent illegal trade is by a collector appointed at home.

8. The natural produce of the province is timber (of various kinds (viz.) (principally) oak, pine, hemlock, ash, beech and birch,) and fish, and they are the only commodity's of the place.

The timber is generally manufactured into beams, plank, knees, boards. clapboards, shingles and staves, and sometimes into house frames, and the value of those commodity's annually exported from hence to Europe and the West-India Islands, is about a thousand pounds sterling. *Mem.* Besides what is above mentioned, the coasting sloops from Boston, carry from hence thither in fish and timber, about five thousand pounds per annum.

9. No mines are yet discovered, except a small quantity of Iron ore in two or three places.

10. The number of inhabitants, men, women and children, are about ten thousand whites, and two hundred blacks.

11. The inhabitants are increased about four thousand within this few years last past, a thousand of which (at least,) are people from Ireland, lately come into, and settled within the province; another reason of the increase of late more than formerly, is a peace with the Indians the four last years.

12. The militia are about eighteen hundred, consisting of two regiments of foot, with a troop of horse in each.

13. There is one fort or place of defence, called Fort William and Mary, situate on the great Island in New-Castle which commands the entrance of Pascataqua river, but is in poor low circumstances, much out of repair, and greatly wanting of stores of war, there not being one barrel of gun-powder, at this time in, or belonging to that garrison.

14. There are no Indians in this province now in time of peace, that we know of.

15. There are no Indians in the neighborhood of this province that we know of, except in the eastern parts of the province of the Massachusetts Bay, and what their number or strength is, we are not acquainted.

16. We have no neighboring Spaniards, or other Europeans, except the French, who, according to the best intelligence we can get, are extremely numerous and strong both at Canada and Cape-Breton.

17. The effect which the French settlements have on this province is, that the Indians are frequently instigated and influenced by them to disturb the peace and quiet of this province, we having been often put to a vast expense both of blood and treasure, to defend ourselves against their cruel outrages.

18. The revenue arising within this province is three hundred ninety and six pounds, by excise, which is appropriated towards the Governor's salary, and about three or four barrels of gun-powder, from the shipping,

which is spent at the fort. There is no other revenue, but by tax on polls and estates.

19. The ordinary expense of the government is about fifteen hundred pounds per annum, now in time of peace; the extraordinary and contingent charges, as repairs of the fort, powder, &c., are about five hundred pounds more.

20. The establishments are six hundred pounds per annum salary on the Governor, eight shillings per diem on each Councillor, and six shillings per diem on each Representative during the session of the general assembly, and a hundred and fifty pounds per annum on the officers, and soldiers at the fort. There is no other establishment civil or military within the government, but the general assembly make allowances from time to time as they see meet, to the Treasurer, Secretary, &c. The Judges, Justices, Sheriffs, Clerks, and all other officers' fees are fixed by a law to be paid by the parties and persons whom they serve, but they have nothing out of the treasury. All the officers, civil and military, hold their places by commission from the Governor, except the Councillors, appointed by the King; the Recorder of deeds, chosen by the general assembly, the Clerks of courts, nominated by the Judges of the said courts respectively, and Selectmen, Assessors, Constables, Tythingmen and other town officers, chosen by the towns, at their respective town meetings.

New-Hampshire Historical Society, *Collections* (Concord, 1824), I, 227-230.

ROBERT ROGERS, "THE RANGER,"
AND HIS DESCENDANTS

This selection indicates the feelings toward Robert Rogers and the pride of the people of New Hampshire.

Source: Mary Cochrane Rogers. <u>Glimpses of An Old Social Capital</u>. Boston: Printed for the Subscribers, 1923.

Robert Rogers, "the Ranger," and His Descendants

ON June 30, 1761, Major Robert Rogers married Elizabeth Browne, youngest and most beautiful daughter of Reverend Arthur Browne, first rector of Queen's Chapel, Portsmouth. Her father performed the marriage ceremony. The bride was dressed in white satin with laces, the same gown in which she sat for her portrait by Joseph Blackburn. There were present on this occasion many stately dames, Copley's living pictures; and gentlemen, too, who may now be seen through the brush of Blackburn and Copley. Just one year, three months, and fifteen days before his daughter Elizabeth became Madam Rogers, Reverend Arthur Browne had made Martha Hilton Lady Wentworth of the Hall. While Parson Browne hesitated at the Wentworth marriage on the Governor's birthday, on this, his daughter's wedding day, he hastened to read the service, and fairly beamed upon his son-in-law.

Major Robert Rogers was twenty-nine years old and had acquired a name and fame in the French and Indian War not eclipsed by any officer then distinguished for valor. Elizabeth was twenty years old, graceful and queen-like. Robert Rogers had met and loved this young girl at the beginning of the "Old French and Indian War." The long trial and delay of their love is charmingly sung by Whittier in his ballad "The Ranger," Robert Rawlin and Martha Mason being no others than Robert Rogers and Elizabeth Browne.

ROBERT RAWLIN!—Frosts were falling
When the ranger's horn was calling
Through the woods to Canada.
Gone the winter's sleet and snowing,
Gone the spring-time's bud and blowing,

Gone the summer's harvest mowing,
  And again the fields are gray.
  Yet away, he's away!
Faint and fainter hope is growing
  In the hearts that mourn his stay.

Where the lion crouching high on
Abraham's rock with teeth of iron,
  Glares o'er wood and wave away,
Faintly thence, as pines far sighing,
Or as thunder spent and dying,
Come the challenge and replying,
  Come the sounds of flight and fray.
  Well-a-day! Hope and pray!
Some are living, some are lying
  In their red graves far away.

Straggling rangers, worn with dangers,
Homeward faring, weary strangers
  Pass the farm-gate on their way;
Tidings of the dead and living,
Forest march and ambush, giving,
Till the maidens leave their weaving,
  And the lads forget their play.
  "Still away, still away!"
Sighs a sad one, sick with grieving,
  "Why does Robert still delay!"

. . . .

"Martha Mason, Martha Mason,
  Prithee tell us of the reason
    Why you mope at home to-day:
  Surely smiling is not sinning;
  Leave your quilting, leave your spinning;
  What is all your store of linen,
    If your heart is never gay?
    Come away, come away!

Never yet did sad beginning
   Make the task of life a play."

. . . .

"Never tell us that you'll fail us,
   Where the purple beach-plum mellows
      On the bluffs so wild and gray.
Hasten, for the oars are falling;
Hark, our merry mates are calling:
Time it is that we were all in,
   Singing tideward down the bay!"
      "Nay, nay, let me stay;
Sore and sad for Robert Rawlin
   Is my heart," she said, "to-day."

"Vain your calling for Rob Rawlin!
   Some red squaw his moose-meat's broiling,
      Or some French lass, singing gay;
Just forget as he's forgetting;
What avails a life of fretting?
If some stars must needs be setting,
   Others rise as good as they."
      "Cease, I pray; go your way!"
Martha cries, her eyelids wetting:
   "Foul and false the words you say!"

"Martha Mason, hear to reason!
   Prithee, put a kinder face on!"
      "Cease to vex me," did she say;
   "Better at his side be lying,
With the mournful pine-trees sighing,
And the wild birds o'er us crying,
   Than to doubt like mine a prey;
      While away, far away,
Turns my heart, forever trying
   Some new hope for each new day.

"When the shadows veil the meadows,
  And the sunset's golden ladders
    Sink from twilight's walls of gray,—
From the window of my dreaming,
I can see his sickle gleaming,
Cheery-voiced, can hear him teaming
    Down the locust-shaded way;
    But away, swift away,
Fades the fond, delusive seeming,
    And I kneel again to pray.

"When the growing dawn is showing,
  And the barn-yard cock is crowing,
    And the horned moon pales away:
From a dream of him awaking,
Every sound my heart is making
Seems a footstep of his taking;
    Then I hush the thought, and say,
    'Nay, nay, he's away!'
Ah! my heart, my heart is breaking
    For the dear one far away."

Look up, Martha! worn and swarthy,
Glows a face of manhood worthy:
  "Robert!" "Martha!" all they say.
O'er went wheel and reel together,
Little cared the owner whither;
Heart of lead is heart of feather,
    Noon of night is noon of day!
    Come away, come away!
When such lovers meet each other,
    Why should prying idlers stay?

PORTSMOUTH'S OLD HOMES

The following is a fine description of the architecture of Portsmouth.

Source: Mary Cochrane Rogers. <u>Glimpses of An Old Social Capital</u>. Boston: Printed for the Subcscribers, 1923.

Portsmouth's Old Homes

NO city in New England is richer in fine old Colonial houses than Portsmouth, New Hampshire. Here and there, scattered along its shaded streets, are some of the finest examples of Colonial architecture to be found, and in most cases they have been preserved in their original beauty. The houses are as alive to-day as they ever were. Now and then some of these old treasure houses are opened to the public for the benefit of St. John's (Arthur Browne's Church, as the people still love to call it), and in the old gardens may be seen descendants of Portsmouth's old families, wandering among the old-fashioned rose beds and arbors, as in the days of yore.

Among the finest examples of architecture is the Governor John Langdon mansion on Pleasant Street, adopted (1907) as a model for a New Hampshire house at the Charleston Exposition. It was erected in 1784 by Governor John Langdon. He was the first president of the United States Senate, and as such informed General Washington of his election as President of the United States. He was five times governor of New Hampshire. Presidents Washington, Monroe, and Taft were entertained in this house. Half-hidden by a magnificent linden tree sits the Wentworth Gardner House, a perfect type of American architecture. This mansion was erected in 1760, by Madam Hunking Wentworth, for her son Thomas. In the kitchen is a large fireplace equipped with an automatic device for roasting meats.

In its setting of graceful elms stands the Warner House, a noted example of early Georgian architecture in America. This mansion was commenced in 1718 and finished in 1723, at an expense of £6000. The brick used in the construction of the eighteen-inch walls was brought from Holland. Over the heavy studded door are two bull's-eye panes of glass. The broad stairway has its walls decorated with original mural paintings, of unknown origin, in perfect condition, representing Governor Phips on his charger, a lady at a spinning-wheel, Abraham offering up Isaac, and numerous other subjects. Once covered by four layers of wall paper, these decorations were accidentally discovered when the removal of a small piece of the paper revealed a painted horse's hoof. In the hall hang enormous elk antlers, presented to the first owner of the house by two Indian friends with whom he dealt in furs. Portraits of these two Indians hang beside them. On the floor of the front room is a carpet which has the distinction of being spotted with wine spilled upon it by Lafayette, a guest at the time. The carpet (despite the wine) is in a remarkable state of preservation, and is still in use. On the walls hang portraits, among them one of Polly Warner by Copley. In a chest may be seen clothes of pre-Revolutionary date — red coats, embroidered long vests, and small-clothes. There is a christening robe made of true cloth of gold. There is an old cocked hat and a sword and a beribboned pair of breeches. Upstairs the beds are all canopied, covered with Revolutionary counterpanes. In one of the chambers is a genuine Franklin stove, one of the few "originals" in existence. Up one side of the Warner House climbs a rusty lightning rod, installed by Benjamin Franklin while visiting Colonel Warner in 1762. This house has never been out of the possession of the family. It has simply passed from one heir to another, without deed. It is entirely furnished with beautiful specimens of early American furniture.

At the end of Little Harbor Road stands the pile of buildings erected by Governor Benning Wentworth in 1750. This mansion is made famous by Longfellow in his ballad of "Lady Wentworth." It was here that the Reverend Arthur Browne in band and gown made Martha Hilton (1760) "Lady Wentworth of the Hall." This house contains thirty-two rooms. In the cellar thirty horses could be stabled in time of danger. The famous Council Chamber, where the King's Council met when Benning Wentworth was governor, is preserved in its original state. The carved mantel-piece above the spacious fire-place, before which Patty Hilton stood on her wedding day gaily attired in rich corn-colored silk, with her hair three stories high, required more than a year's time of a wood-carver's chisel. On the walls once hung a valuable portrait, painted by Copley, of the lovely Dorothy Quincy, who married John Hancock and afterwards became Madam Scott. This lady was a niece of Dr. Holmes's "Dorothy Q." Despite the discrepancy in age—forty years—Lady Wentworth turned out to be a faultless wife, and Governor Wentworth signified his approval of her by leaving her his entire estate at his death in 1770. The period of mourning was very brief, however—two months—for that same year she married again, this time Colonel Michael Wentworth, a retired officer of the British Army, who came to this country in 1767. He fixed his residence at Little Harbor and soon dissipated his wife's fortune in high living. He died suddenly in New York—it was said by his own hand. The last words attributed to him were, "I have had my cake, and ate it." The death of one of Portsmouth's most distinguished daughters is thus recorded in the *Oracle*, published Saturday, December 28, 1805:

"Died in this town on Wednesday last after a short illness which she bore with great fortitude and entire resignation to the Divine Will, Madam Martha Wentworth relict of the late Col. Michael Wentworth, aged 67.

"The funeral will take place this afternoon and move from the house of the late Judge [Woodbury] Langdon at three o'clock."

Colonel Michael and Martha Hilton Wentworth had one child, named Martha. The harpsichord in the Council Chamber belonged to Martha Wentworth. Long after the Revolution she married Sir

John Wentworth, a nephew of Governor John Wentworth, and resided for some time in the mansion at Little Harbor. She died in London in 1852.

It is interesting to note that the rich corn-colored silk gown worn by Martha Hilton was preserved and became the wedding gown of a direct descendant—Mrs. William Alexander, of Philadelphia.

On Livermore Street stands the Livermore Mansion, erected by Matthew Livermore about 1735, on the present Haven Park, fronting on Pleasant Street. Samuel Livermore, called "the great man of New Hampshire" in his time, lived here during the administration of Governor John Wentworth. Although this house has had two removals, it stands to-day a fine example of Colonial architecture.

Shaded by horse-chestnut trees stands the Moffatt-Ladd House. This delightful old building is the home of the Society of the Colonial Dames of New Hampshire. It was built in 1763, by Captain John Moffatt, commander of one of the King's ships carrying masts from Kittery Point to England. It became the home of General William Whipple, a son-in-law, who was elected a member of the Continental Congress in 1775, and who was a signer of the Declaration of Independence. This mansion came into the possession of Alexander Ladd and his wife, whose descendants transferred it to the Society of Colonial Dames for twenty years. The building is of unusual architectural interest. The hall is a reproduction of a hall in the house of Captain Moffatt's father in England. Some of the wood carvings were done by Grinling Gibbons. The house is furnished in Colonial style. In the rear is a delightful old garden, with arbors, terraces, lawns, and walks bordered by flowers of our great-great-grandmother's day.

On Court Street is the home of Mr. Winslow Pierce, a large and fine structure with a graceful cupola. This house was either built by McIntire or in his style, in the early nineteenth century. It has never been out of the family. Its chief attraction is a spiral staircase that ascends from the entrance hall, winding up for three stories. And in the ceiling above the stairs is a delicate white medallion. A closet contains old china, and a cupboard, fans, watches, and rings. The woodwork is unusually delicate, and is all hand-carved.

On Pleasant Street stands the Jacob Wendell House, built about 1765. A charming enclosed garden extends within a series of enclosed courtyards far in the rear. Since 1817 it has been in the Wendell family, nor has any division of property ever taken place. All the furniture and effects of the five Wendell generations have been preserved there. Many of the pieces date back to 1750. Within, decorated window shades, an ancient piano, an old fire screen, and pieces of old glass and chinaware delight the interested visitor. One obtains here certainly more than a glimpse into the past.

The Spencer House on State Street dates from 1763, and has been occupied at various times by the Portsmouth families of Parrot, Pickering, and Whipple. Its chief feature is a magnificent staircase, to which nearly the whole lower floor is sacrificed. Unusual combinations of white painted wood and natural mahogany add to its beauty by contrast. Behind the house is a garden which contains a number of arched bowers, through which a view of the finely proportioned door can be had.

There are three buildings in Portsmouth attributed to Bulfinch: the Portsmouth Public Library; the Larkin House of red brick with beautiful Palladian windows, built in 1813; and the Portsmouth Athenaeum, established as a library by act of Legislature in 1817. The Athenaeum contains a valuable collection of early books, and is especially rich in rare prints and pamphlets of early provincial days. It has received many valuable legacies. Among them were those of Benjamin T. Tredick, of Philadelphia, and Charles Levi Woodbury, of Boston. It contains paintings of Sir Peter Warren, done in 1751, and of Sir William Pepperrell, who led the New England forces at Louisburg in 1745. There are also pictures and models of ships, and an order of George II in Council appointing a committee to assemble at Hampton to adjust the boundaries between New Hampshire and Massachusetts Bay. Two British cannon flank the front door. An Admiralty model of the British 74-gun ship "America," built under the supervision of John Paul Jones on Badger's Island, is one of the treasures of the Athenaeum.

The porches and front doors of many of these old Portsmouth dwellings have long been recognized as the most interesting Colonial architecture existing in the country.

The End

NEW HAMPSHIRE SOCIAL LIFE

The selections printed below present a fine description of life among the upper classes during the eighteenth and nineteenth centuries.

Source: Mary Cochrane Rogers. *Glimpses of an Old Social Capital*. Boston: Printed for the Subscribers, 1923.

ONE hundred years ago, and something more,
In Queen Street, Portsmouth, at her tavern door,
Neat as a pin, and blooming as a rose,
Stood Mistress Stavers in her furbelows,
Just as her cuckoo-clock was striking nine.
Above her head, resplendent on the sign,
The portrait of the Earl of Halifax,
In scarlet coat and periwig of flax,
Surveyed at leisure all her varied charms,
Her cap, her bodice, her white folded arms,
And half resolved, though he was past his prime,
And rather damaged by the lapse of time,
To fall down at her feet, and to declare
The passion that had driven him to despair.
For from his lofty station he had seen
Stavers, her husband, dressed in bottle-green,
Drive his new Flying Stage-coach, four in hand,
Down the long lane, and out into the land.
And knew that he was far upon the way
To Ipswich and to Boston on the Bay!

Just then the meditations of the Earl
Were interrupted by a little girl,
Barefooted, ragged, with neglected hair,
Eyes full of laughter, neck and shoulders bare,
A thin slip of a girl, like a new moon,
Sure to be rounded into beauty soon,

A creature men would worship and adore,
Though now in mean habiliments she bore
A pail of water dripping, through the street,
And bathing, as she went, her naked feet.

It was a pretty picture, full of grace,—
The slender form, the delicate, thin face;
The swaying motion, as she hurried by;
The shining feet, the laughter in her eye,
That o'er her face in ripples gleamed and glanced,
As in her pail the shifting sunbeam danced:
And with uncommon feelings of delight
The Earl of Halifax beheld the sight.
Not so Dame Stavers, for he heard her say
These words, or thought he did, as plain as day:
"O Martha Hilton! Fie! how dare you go
About the town half dressed, and looking so!"
At which the gypsy laughed, and straight replied:
"No matter how I look; I yet shall ride
In my own chariot, ma'am." And on the child
The Earl of Halifax benignly smiled,
As with her heavy burden she passed on,
Looked back, then turned the corner, and was gone.

What next, upon that memorable day,
Arrested his attention was a gay
And brilliant equipage, that flashed and spun,
The silver harness glittering in the sun,
Outriders with red jackets, lithe and lank,
Pounding the saddles as they rose and sank,
While all alone within the chariot sat
A portly person with three-cornered hat,
A crimson velvet coat, head high in air,
Gold-headed cane, and nicely powdered hair,
And diamond buckles sparkling at his knees,
Dignified, stately, florid, much at ease.

Onward the pageant swept, and as it passed,
Fair Mistress Stavers courtesied low and fast;
For this was Governor Wentworth, driving down
To Little Harbor, just beyond the town,
Where his Great House stood looking out to sea,
A goodly place, where it was good to be.

It was a pleasant mansion, an abode
Near and yet hidden from the great high-road,
Sequestered among trees, a noble pile,
Baronial and colonial in its style;
Gables and dormer-windows everywhere,
And stacks of chimneys rising high in air,—
Pandæan pipes, on which all winds that blew
Made mournful music the whole winter through.
Within, unwonted splendors met the eye,
Panels, and floors of oak, and tapestry;
Carved chimney-pieces, where on brazen dogs
Revelled and roared the Christmas fires of logs;
Doors opening into darkness unawares,
Mysterious passages, and flights of stairs;
And on the walls, in heavy gilded frames,
The ancestral Wentworths, with Old-Scripture names.

Such was the mansion where the great man dwelt,
A widower and childless; and he felt
The loneliness, the uncongenial gloom,
That like a presence haunted every room;
For though not given to weakness, he could feel
The pain of wounds, that ache because they heal.

The years came and the years went,—seven in all,
And passed in cloud and sunshine o'er the Hall;
The dawns their splendor through its chambers shed,
The sunsets flushed its western windows red;
The snow was on its roofs, the wind, the rain;
Its woodlands were in leaf and bare again;

Moons waxed and waned, the lilacs bloomed and died,
In the broad river ebbed and flowed the tide,
Ships went to sea, and ships came home from sea,
And the slow years sailed by and ceased to be.

And all these years had Martha Hilton served
In the Great House, not wholly unobserved:
By day, by night, the silver crescent grew,
Though hidden by clouds, her light still shining through;
A maid of all work, whether coarse or fine,
A servant who made service seem divine!
Through her each room was fair to look upon;
The mirrors glistened, and the brasses shone,
The very knocker on the outer door,
If she but passed, was brighter than before.

And now the ceaseless turning of the mill
Of Time, that never for an hour stands still,
Ground out the Governor's sixtieth birthday,
And powdered his brown hair with silver-gray.
The robin, the forerunner of the spring,
The bluebird with his jocund carolling,
The restless swallows building in the eaves,
The golden buttercups, the grass, the leaves,
The lilacs tossing in the winds of May,
All welcomed this majestic holiday!
He gave a splendid banquet, served on plate,
Such as became the Governor of the State,
Who represented England and the King,
And was magnificent in everything.
He had invited all his friends and peers,
The Pepperels, the Langdons, and the Lears,
The Sparhawks, the Penhallows, and the rest;
For why repeat the name of every guest?
But I must mention one, in bands and gown,
The rector there, the Reverend Arthur Brown

Of the Established Church; with smiling face
He sat beside the Governor and said grace;
And then the feast went on, as others do,
But ended as none other I e'er knew.

When they had drunk the King, with many a cheer,
The Governor whispered in a servant's ear,
Who disappeared, and presently there stood
Within the room, in perfect womanhood,
A maiden, modest and yet self-possessed,
Youthful and beautiful, and simply dressed.
Can this be Martha Hilton? It must be!
Yes, Martha Hilton, and no other she!
Dowered with the beauty of her twenty years,
How ladylike, how queenlike she appears;
The pale, thin crescent of the days gone by
Is Dian now in all her majesty!
Yet scarce a guest perceived that she was there,
Until the Governor, rising from his chair,
Played slightly with his ruffles, then looked down,
And said unto the Reverend Arthur Brown:
"This is my birthday: it shall likewise be
My wedding-day; and you shall marry me!"

The listening guests were greatly mystified,
None more so than the rector, who replied:
"Marry you? Yes, that were a pleasant task,
Your Excellency; but to whom? I ask."
The Governor answered: "To this lady here";
And beckoned Martha Hilton to draw near.
She came and stood, all blushes, at his side.
The rector paused. The impatient Governor cried:
"This is the lady; do you hesitate?
Then I command you as Chief Magistrate."
The rector read the service loud and clear:
"Dearly beloved, we are gathered here,"

NEW HAMPSHIRE AND THE FEDERAL JUDICIARY, 1794 - 1795

The following remonstrances of the state of New Hampshire in regard to a decision of the United States Circuit Court for the District of New Hampshire indicates the many concerns over the powers of the federal courts as exercised in regard to the activities of the states.

Source: Herman V. Ames, ed. *State Documents on Federal Relations: The States and the United States.* Philadelphia: Published by the Department of History of the University of Pennsylvania, 1906.

New Hampshire and the Federal Judiciary.
1794, 1795.

The first of the following remonstrances was due to a decision rendered by the United States Circuit Court for the District of New Hampshire, October 24, 1793, enforcing the decree of the Court of Appeals in Cases of Capture, in a case growing out of the capture of the brigantine "*Susannah*" by the privateer the "*McClary*" in October, 1777. The latter vessel was owned and manned by citizens of New Hampshire, but was acting under the commission and authority of Congress. The Courts of New Hampshire condemned the "*Susannah*" and her cargo as lawful prize, and refused to grant an appeal to Congress as contrary to the law of the State. A petition for an appeal in this case (*Treadwell and Penhallow v. brig Susannah*) was, however, sent to Congress, and its prayer granted by the Court of Commissioners, June 26, 1779, by virtue of the Resolves of Congress of November 25, 1775 (*Journal of Congress* [ed. 1800], I, 241, 242.) The case came up for trial before the legal successors of this body, the newly erected Court of Appeals in Cases of Capture (Resolves of January 15, 1780, *Jour. of Cong.*, VI, 10) in September, 1783. This Court reversed the decision of the New Hampshire Courts. Here the case rested until Elisha Doane, one of the appellants, finally brought proceedings in the Federal Circuit Court of New Hampshire in 1793, with the result as indicated above. On a writ of error the case was brought before the Supreme Court of the United States, and judgment was given, February 24, 1795, in the case of *Penhallow et al., v. Doane's Administrators*, maintaining the jurisdiction of the United States Courts, and confirming the decision of the inferior courts. The second of these remonstrances was presented to Congress three days later.

References: Texts: *Amer. State Papers, Misc.*, I, 79, 123, 124. See the case of *Penhallow v. Doane*, 3 *Dallas*, 54, for full facts in the case. For history of the United States Courts prior to the adoption of the Constitution, and incidentally of this case, see J. F. Jameson, *The Predecessor of the Supreme Court*, in *Essays in Const. History*, ch. 1; J. C. Bancroft Davis, *Courts of Appeal in Prize Cases*, 131 *United States Reports*, Appx. xxix-xxxiv.

First Remonstrance of the Legislature, February 20, 1794.

State of New Hampshire:

To the Senate and House of Representatives of the United States in Congress assembled: The remonstrance of the Legislature of the State of New Hampshire, showeth:—

That the citizens of the State of New Hampshire adopted the federal constitution of the United States under the full conviction that more extensive general powers were necessary to be vested in Congress than they ever possessed or pretended that they possessed, when they were entirely dependent on the good-will or the resolves of the several States. But by this adoption they did not then intend, nor does their Legislature now choose to admit, that the confederation was in force prior to March, 1781, or that the federal constitution existed with respect to New Hampshire before June, 1788. That a question respecting the powers of Congress and the powers of the several States previous to the constitution or the confederation has been determined in the circuit court for the district of New Hampshire, held at Exeter on the 24th day of October, 1793, in which the foundation of the action was, whether this State, prior to an express grant to Congress, had a right to pass a law final in every way concerning the capture of vessels by this State, or citizens thereof, from the British, the enemy we were then engaged with in war. That the determination of this circuit court was, that the State of New Hampshire had no such power; but that Congress, or a court commissioned by them, could nullify the laws of any particular State; could control their several courts; and that in fact, the constitution of 1789 was unnecessary to be adopted, as it contained no new grant of powers, but only a confirmation of old ones.

* * * * * * *

The states are forbidden by the federal constitution to make any retrospective laws. The Legislature conceived that Congress was under the same obligations; and that their courts could not rejudge cases that were finally adjudged by courts existing prior to its adoption. In fact, the Legislature conceive, and feel no inclination to relinquish the idea, that Congress, in its origin, was merely an advisory body, chosen by the several States to consult upon measures for the general good of the whole; that the adoption of measures recommended by them was entirely in the breast of the several States or their Legislatures; that no measure could be carried into effect in any State without its agreement thereto; that the subsequent powers of Congress entirely depended upon the express grants of the State Legislatures; that the Legislature of this State, so far from agreeing to the exercise of the power by Congress or its courts, now determined by the circuit court to have belonged to them, on request from Congress, did not grant, but denied it; that the declaration of independence received effect from its being acceded to by the Legislatures of the several States; and that the confederation was the first act binding upon the States which was not expressly agreed to by them individually; that a declaration by any body whatever contrary thereto is subversive of the principles of the revolution; unsettling all the proceedings of the State Governments prior to the existence of the constitution; and will inevitably involve the States, and this State in particular, in confusion, and will weaken, if not perhaps destroy, the National Government; the true principles of which the State of New Hampshire has, and will always endeavor to maintain.

The Legislature of New Hampshire, therefore, again protest and remonstrate against the exercise of any such powers by Congress, or any court or body of men appointed by them, and request that measures may be taken to prevent and annihilate such illegal acts of power.

6. Second Remonstrance of the Legislature, January 16, 1795.

To the Senate and House of Representatives of the United States in Congress assembled: The Memorial of the Legislature of New Hampshire, showeth:

That impelled by a firm attachment to the first principles of a free Government, and the accumulated distresses of a number of their citizens, they again remonstrate to Congress against a violation of State independence and an unwarrantable encroachment in the courts of the United States.

[Here follows a statement of the case as they view it.]

That this State had a right to oppose the British usurpation in the way it thought best; could make laws as it chose, with respect to every transaction where it had not explicitly granted the power to Congress; that the formation of courts for carrying those laws into execution belonged only to the several States; that Congress might advise and recommend, but the States only could enact and carry into execution; and that the attempts repeatedly made to render the laws of this State in this respect null and void is a flagrant insult to the principle of the revolution; is establishing a Government they hoped to be a blessing on the uniform plea of arbitrary power, on an implication of grants of jurisdiction not intended to be included, nor even in contemplation.

Can the rage for annihilating all the power of the States, and reducing this extensive and flourishing country to one domination, make the administrators blind to the danger of violating all the principles of our former Government, to the hazard of convulsions in endeavoring to eradicate every trace of State power, except in the resentment of the people? Can the constitutional exercise of the power of Congress in future be in no other way established than by the belief that the former Congress always possessed the same? Can the remembrance of the manner of our opposition to tyranny, and the gradual adoption of federal ideas, be so painful as to exclude (unless forced into view) the knowledge that Congress, in its origin, was merely an advisory body; that it entirely depended upon the will of the several Legislatures to enforce any measure they might recommend; that the inconveniences of this principle produced the confederation; and, even at that late day, it was declared that powers not expressly delegated to Congress are reserved to the States, or the people, respectively; that the experience of years, of the inefficacy of thirteen Legislatures to provide for the wants and to procure the happiness of the American people, caused the adoption of the present constitution—an adoption totally unnecessary, in point of principle, if the claims of former Congressional power are established.

Forced by events, the Legislature of New Hampshire have made the foregoing statements; and while they cheerfully acknowledge the power of Congress in cases arising under the constitution, they equally resolve not to submit the laws, made before the existence of the present government by this (then independent State) to the adjudication of any power on earth, while the freedom of the Federal Government shall afford any constitutional means of redress

Impressed with the singular merits of the present case, and deprecating the many and complicated evils which must be the necessary consequence of establishing the power claimed by the courts of the United States, and its tendency to produce disaffection to our Government, the Legislature of New Hampshire rest assured that a speedy and just decision will be had, and that the rights of State Governments and the interests of their citizens will be secured against the exercise of a power of a court, or any body of men under Congress, of carrying into effect an unconstitutional decree of a court instituted by a former Congress, and which, in its effects, would unsettle property and tear up the laws of the several states.

WHITTIER'S NEW HAMPSHIRE

Using Whittier's poetry as a starting point, the author describes the various beauties of the state and also presents quotations from many authors to illustrate the fine qualities of the state.

Source: David Lee Maulsby, "Whittier's New Hampshire," The New England Magazine. New Series, vol. XXII, August, 1900.

WHITTIER'S NEW HAMPSHIRE.

By David Lee Maulsby.

THE fashionable world has elected to make its summer pilgrimage to the White Mountains; and to this day the Presidential range and its neighborhood are the objective points for most admiring tourists in New Hampshire. But Whittier's favorite haunts were to the south of the parallel belonging to Sandwich Notch, through which, one autumn day, "the west wind sang good morrow to the cotter"; and "Chocorua's horn" was to him, so far as his pages show, more impressive than the rocky summit of Mount Washington. It is true that during the last twelve years of his life the Quaker singer was from time to time a summer guest at Intervale; but these later years have left small record in his verse. It is also true that, near the beginning of his poetical career, his rather long poem, "The Bridal of Pennacook," was written in northern New Hampshire, in order, characteristically enough, to soothe the waking hours of an invalid girl. The name of Passaconaway, the Indian chief whose daughter is the heroine of this poem, is now associated once for all with the beautiful dome-like mountain of the Sandwich range. Clearly this Indian chief was a favorite hero of Whittier's, for "Passaconaway" was the title of a prose tale that he wrote before 1839, the scene of which was laid on the banks of the Merrimac River.

It was in the valley of the Pemigewasset that N. P. Rogers lived, whom Whittier visited with pleasure when only twenty-six years old, and who later entertained the famous English antislavery agitator, George Thompson. In Concord, New Hampshire, it will be remembered, Whittier and his English friend, after a speech by the latter, were threatened with death by a bloodthirsty mob. In his appreciative sketch of Mr. Rogers, Whittier makes many loving references to New Hampshire scenery; for example: "One can almost see the sunset light flooding the Franconia Notch and glorifying the peaks of Moosehillock, and hear the murmur of the west wind in the pines, and the light, liquid voice of Pemigewasset sounding up from its rocky channel, through its green hem of maples."

Related to the same vicinity is the beautiful apostrophe to the summits of the North, in "Mountain Pictures." The boldness of the following lines, afterwards tamed into acceptable conformity at the suggestion of another, is noteworthy:

"Last night's thunder-gust
Roared not in vain; for where its lightnings thrust
Their tongues of fire, the great peaks seem so near,
Lapped clear of mist . . ."

Mrs. Fields tells sympathetically of a visit paid her in Campton in 1865, when the poet, beginning with Emerson's pregnant lines upon "The Sphinx," discoursed upon the mysteries of spiritual existence, and ended by recounting a vision concerning the outcome of the civil war, described in writing by an old man of Sandwich a quarter of a century before the event.

Another region of New Hampshire connected with Whittier's writings is the southeastern part, near his Amesbury home, and bordering upon the ocean. Whittier's associations with the Isles of Shoals have already been described in the NEW ENGLAND MAGAZINE.* The "Ramoth Hill" of that heart-revealing poem, "My Playmate," was in Hampton. In the same place General Moulton used to live, a legend connected with whose family appears in "The New Wife and the Old." The ancestors of the Hugh Tallant who planted "The Sycamores" came from Ireland to settle in New Hampshire. At Seabrook lived Elizabeth Gove of peaceful memory.

"Her path shall brighten more and more
Unto the perfect day;
She cannot fail of peace who bore
Such peace with her away."†

It was at the house of Sarah Gove, at Hampton Falls, that at last the tired singer gently slipped away from life.

But Whittier's memory, as did his love, clings most closely about that part of New Hampshire which lies, on the map, below Campton and above Laconia. And, indeed, when full recognition is given to his affection for the part of the Granite State which is nearest to his Massachusetts home, and when all is said in due praise of the giant mountains of the north, it is not surprising that Whittier dearly loved the milder central region. For the country about Lake Winnepesaukee, if it does not lie stretched at the feet of great mountainous masses of towering height, is yet full of the calmer beauty of hills and vales diversified with sheets of water, now placid as a mirror, now white-capped by the breeze. In sight, too, from favorable points are many of the eminent sentinels of time—half the horizon, it may be, rimmed with distant peak behind peak. Thus, from a convenient high point on the stage road between Moultonboro and Sandwich, one can see Chocorua, Paugus, Passaconaway, Wonalancet, Whiteface, Tripyramid, Black Mountain (sometimes inappropriately called Sandwich Dome), and Mount Israel, to say nothing of the less conspicuous Squam Mountains, extending toward the west. The reader of early American war ballads will recall that rude description of Lovewell's fight, when Paugus, chief of the Pigwacket Indians, was attacked by "worthy Captain Lovewell." But one's pleasure in the view need not be complicated with historico-literary associations. Let him rather turn to the left, where Red Hill lifts its several summits to heaven.

"So seemed it when yon hill's red crown,
Of old, the Indian trod,
And, through the sunset air, looked down
Upon the Smile of God."

Or he may turn to the right, where Ossipee Mountain, with its Black Snout, shows its long ridge.

"The shadows round the inland sea
Are deepening into night;
Slow up the slopes of Ossipee
They chase the lessening light."

"Tired of the long day's blinding heat,
I rest my languid eye,
Lake of the hills! where, cool and sweet,
Thy sunset waters lie!" *

Red Hill might conveniently be encompassed in half a day's good driving; but the roots of Ossipee extend in so many directions that one with the best horse could hardly encircle all of them in a single sweep, should one travel from sunrise till the fall of evening. Even Black Snout is celebrated, as the reader may see if he will turn to the third stanza of "A Letter," published anonymously during the heated political contest of 1846, when John P. Hale of New Hampshire was elected to the United States Senate to the joy of the abolitionists.

What wonderful changes the poet saw pass over his beloved mountains; what shadows of clouds on their breasts, while the concealed sun spread broad fields of light below; what mists lazily rose from slope to slope, or clung like a wreath upon the half-hidden hoary head! What sun-

---

* In the article, "In Whittier Land," by W. S. Kennedy, November, 1892.

† "The Friend's Burial."

* "The Lakeside."

sets painted their fascinating or grotesque shapes of color, while the land lay slumbering in a tender radiance, as of a life well spent and drawing to its peaceful close! There was something congenial to Whittier's disposition in the tempered boldness of this landscape, its glimpses of possessing beauty, its virile restraint.

Of the score or more of poems suggested to Whittier while he was in the Granite State, the greater part represent one or another of three localities, —the Bearcamp River, Asquam (or Squam) Lake, and Lake Winnepesaukee. All three of these regions may be included in a square, the side of which measures twenty-five miles. For many happy summers the inn at West Ossipee was the accustomed place of meeting for Whittier and his friends, among whom Lucy Larcom may be particularly mentioned as a fellow worker in letters. Here the poet, with his group of associates, young and old, gathered about the evening fireside, would listen with zest to the tale of the day's adventures, and join heartily in the merriment of the hour. For among his intimate friends, Whittier's reputation as a teller of stories and a maker of pleasant talk almost equals his reputation as a poet. The name of the hostelry thus made fragrant with happy memories was the Bearcamp House, although Whittier, in his prefatory note to the "Voyage of the Jettie," speaks of it as the "Wayside Inn." It was burned down in 1881, much to the poet's regret. All that is now left of it is the cellar-place, overgrown with a tangle of bushes. But the peaceful street of the village remains, and over it one of the two new inns hangs out its picturesque sign-board of Revolutionary fashion, while the other extends to the visitor the welcoming arms of its broad piazza. The Bearcamp River winds along the roadway in its stony channel, and can be traced in its meandering for many miles. Of literary interest is the traditional spot near the covered bridge, whence the *Jettie*, named in honor of "the Bay State's graceful daughter," Mrs. Jettie Morrill Wason, was launched.

"On she glided, overladen,
  With merry man and maiden
    Sending back their song and laughter,
While, perchance, a phantom crew,
In a ghostly birch canoe,
    Paddled dumb and swiftly after!"

"All the pines that o'er her hung
In mimic sea-tones sung
  The song familiar to her;
And the maples leaned to screen her,
And the meadow grass seemed greener,
  And the breeze more soft to woo her!"

"Dies now the gay persistence
Of song and laugh in distance;
  Alone with me remaining
The stream, the quiet meadow,
The hills in shine and shadow,
  The sombre pines complaining."

At the request of the same lady, who also first sang it, was composed the love song, "The Henchman," by no means so much read as it deserves. It is hard to resist the impression that the unfulfilled love which found expression in "My Playmate," and in "Memories," and which perhaps is hinted in the concluding stanza of "Maud Muller," was also the inspiration of this mediæval picture of a self-effacing lover, forever faithful, seeking no sign that his lady shares his passion.

There are other unpublished poems relating to the shores of the Bearcamp, and at least two such poems that have been published. "How They Climbed Chocorua" belongs to the former group, and humorously celebrates the adventures of seven of the poet's young friends, who spent the night on the horned mountain. The Knox brothers, who were accustomed to furnish bear steaks to the inn, acted as guides in this adventure, and the poem celebrating the ascent was read by Lucy Larcom at a husking in the Knox barn, not far from the inn, soon after the party returned. The poem was read as coming from an unknown writer, although everybody knew that Whittier, who sat silently by, must be the author. As a reward, the poet was presented with the bear skin that was then stretching on the barn door.

Of the two published poems that relate to the Bearcamp country, one deserves a word by itself. The inquisitive sojourner in West Ossipee is likely to find himself confused in his attempts to discover historical basis for that popular narrative poem, "Among the Hills." Surely Whittier never wrote a better bit of description than this:

"The locust by the wall
Stabs the noon-silence with his sharp alarm;"

and the rest of the prelude is noteworthy as containing a plea for beauty in the humblest life. The body of the poem, as many readers will remember, begins with the description of a brilliant autumn day, presaging winter, while filled with memories of June.

"Above his broad lake, Ossipee,
Once more the sunshine wearing,
Stooped, tracing on that silver shield
His grim armorial bearing."

In the afternoon of this glorious day, made more resplendent by contrast with the preceding weeks of rain, the poet is driving, "my hostess at my side," on an errand that takes them to a certain white farmhouse,

"Where taste had wound its arms of vines
Round thrift's uncomely rudeness."

"The sun-brown farmer in his frock
Shook hands, and called to Mary:
Bare-armed, as Juno might, she came,
White-aproned from her dairy.

"Her air, her smile, her motions, told
Of womanly completeness;
A music as of household songs
Was in her voice of sweetness."

On the way home the hostess tells how this cultivated wife came to be in the honest farmer's home:

"From school and ball and rout she came,
The city's fair, pale daughter,
To drink the wine of mountain air
Beside the Bearcamp Water!"

She tells how her step grew firm and cheeks blooming.

"For health comes sparkling in the streams
From cool Chocorua stealing;
There's iron in our northern winds,
Our pines are trees of healing."

The farmer straightway falls in love with the beautiful city maiden, who playfully puts aside his advances until his passionate rejoinder convinces her that his life happiness depends upon her answer. Then she gracefully avows that she loves him. The result is a marriage that establishes the maiden among the mountains, a centre of refinement and a revealer of nature's loveliness to those who have hitherto been unseeing.

"The coarseness of a ruder time
Her finer mirth displaces,
A subtler sense of pleasure fills
Each rustic sport she graces.

"Her presence lends its warmth and health
To all who come before it.
If woman lost us Eden, such
As she alone restore it."

The farmer becomes prosperous, and in due time is sent as representative to the General Court.

The verisimilitude of such details naturally provokes inquiry. "Who was the sun-brown farmer?" Who in real life was the city bred "Mary" that he wedded, each thus experiencing, in their perfect union, "the giving that is gaining"? And who was the "hostess," who told the story so circumstantially to the poet, as he drove at evening by her side to buy some butter from the proud housewife? More than one student has tried to answer these questions, and has weighed the probabilities which attach to the legend each one of the neighboring farmers who married maidens from the city. Now and then, some misguided questioner, by letter or by personal interview, has made inquiry of those patient women, who, at one time or another, served as hostess of the old Bearcamp River House. Some wielders of the modern camera have even carried off in triumph a photograph of house or gravestone, hugging it as an authentic memento. But, so far as the heroine of the poem is concerned, Whittier's own words set the matter forever at rest. In a letter written shortly after the burning of the Bearcamp House he says: "The lady of the poem 'Among the Hills' was purely imaginary. I was charmed with the scenery in Tamworth and West Ossipee, and tried to call attention to it in a story." This letter is given at page 669 of Mr. Pickard's biography, to which friends of Whittier must always be deeply indebted. In the earliest version of the poem, the landlord, not the landlady, tells the story.

Before leaving the region of West Ossipee and Tamworth, it is worth remarking that three mountains have, at one time or another, laid claim to Whittier as godfather. As one may see on recent maps, the two noble hills in South Tamworth, whose bases may be said to meet, while their sky-lines are quite distinct, are called Whittier and Larcom, and thus fitly typify the friendship and fellowship of their namesakes. Formerly the mountain now called Larcom was called Whittier. But the late Mr. M.F. Sweetser, who named this mountain for the Quaker poet, consented to the change of name proposed by the Appalalchian Club, and when the matter was left to a vote of the people of Tamworth, in town meeting assembled, they approved the new name, "Larcom," which, in consequence, as it now appears upon the maps, is sufficiently authorized while "Whittier" appropriately designates the larger and loftier of these two neighboring mountains. The third claimant of the poet as godfather is a pretty hill in West Ossipee, whose ascending path starts not far from the launching place of the *Jettie*. Once up the hill the climber, gets an entrancing view of the valley of the Bearcamp, such as might well suggest a loving description like that in "Sunset on the Bearcamp":

"A gold fringe on the purpling hem
  Of hills, the river runs,
As down its long green valley falls
  The last of summer's suns.
Along its tawny gravel-bed
  Broad flowing, swift and still,
As if its meadow levels felt
  The hurry of the hill,
Noiseless between its banks of green
  From curve to curve it slips;
The drowsy maple-shadows rest
  Like fingers on its lips."

"Touched by a light that hath no name,
  A glory never sung,
Aloft on sky and mountain wall
  Are God's great pictures hung."

The local tradition is that Whittier used to climb the hill, by no means an impossible task for an active man of sixty-nine; but the Quaker bard was a semi-invalid during his successive summers in this place, and at the date of the poem was accustomed to let his younger friends go mountain climbing without him.

Several summers were spent in part at the Asquam House, in Holderness, on the summit of Shepard Hill. It was at the Asquam House that the lines on the death of Longfellow were written in a volume of his poems. It was from the veranda of the house that Whittier watched the progress of the tempest limned in powerful lines in his "Storm on Lake Asquam," and it was from the same inn that the following letter was sent to Mrs. Fields:

"Thy dear letter comes to me here, and I have read it where this beautiful but unhistoric lake stretches away before me, greengemmed with islands, until it loses itself in the purple haze of the Gunstock Mountains, whose summits redden in the setting sun . . . . I left Amesbury yesterday in a hot southerly rainstorm; but just as we reached Alton Bay the wind shifted to the north-northeast and blew a gale, scattering the clouds, and by the time our steamer passed out of the bay into the lake the water was white-capped, and waves broke heavily on the small islands, flinging their foam and spray against the green foliage on the shores. It was pleasant to see again the rugged mass of Ossipee loom up before us, and the familiar shapes of the long Sandwich range come slowly into view. To-day the weather is perfect,—clear keen sunshine, and cool, bracing wind. The season is rather late, and the sweetbrier roses are still in bloom, and these often parched hill slopes are now green as your English downs."

The Gunstock Mountains mentioned above, or "peaks of Gunstock," as the twin summits were otherwise called, are now united as Mount Belknap.

At Asquam Lake, Whittier met gladly some of General Armstrong's teachers from the Hampton Institute in Virginia, and to this region he would urge his friends to come to visit him ere it should be too late. He never tired of the Asquam Lakes, in storm and sunshine, and speaks of them as "the loveliest lakes of New England." Again, he says: "Such a sunset the Lord never before painted." The summit of Shepard Hill, upon which the Asquam House stands, affords outlook to the horizon on every side. In "The Hilltop," one aspect of the view is thus described:

"There towered Chocorua's peak;
  and west,
Moosehillock's woods were seen,
With many a nameless slide-scarred
  crest
And pine-dark gorge between.
Beyond them, like a sun-rimmed cloud,
  The great Notch mountains shone,
Watched over by the solemn-browed
  And awful face of stone!"

Our shy poet abandoned this wide prospect only when the crowds of curious visitors became annoying to him.

It may seem strange to those who have visited but one of these places that Whittier preferred the Asquam lakes to the outlook from Ossipee Park, high up on Ossipee Mountain. The lofty plateau is commanding, the sight satisfying of Winnepesaukee, and its dotting islands, with perchance a glimpse of the lake steamboat, the *Mount Washington*, tiny in the distance, emitting its ribbon of smoke. Grandly impressive is the rocky gorge, carved by the streams of centuries, spanned by many rustic bridges, which overlook cascades and silent stony pools. When Whittier visited Ossipee Park in 1884, he was too feeble to climb up and down the steep pathways, and could not have gone so far as the chief cataract. Nor did he thrust his hand into that rocky cave known as "the devil's den," in which His Satanic Majesty might still take refuge, if he were now no larger than the serpent that tempted Eve. But there was a seat the Quaker poet loved, where he could muse upon a waterfall as it slipped from pool to pool, under a leaning leafy birch near "Mary's Arch," and there still hangs a painted piece of wood bearing the year and day of his reverie.

It may have been this ascent of Ossipee Mountain that he had in mind when he said that he had once looked down upon the scene from another mountain and found that it had lost its charm. But it is certain that the lake whose Indian name he had written meant "the Smile of God," was a lasting source of rest and inspiration. It is commemorated in at least four of his poems: "The Lakeside," "Summer by the Lakeside," "A Summer Pilgrimage," and "A Legend of the Lake." Whittier, in his later years, used to like the hotel at Centre Harbor, partly because of its earlier associations with his sister Elizabeth. No doubt there are "summer people" at Centre Harbor, who, treading the shores of Winnepesaukee, pass the site of the deed celebrated in the last-named poem without being aware of it. On the other hand, scarcely a week of the summer goes by without some one stopping at the home of " 'Squire Dow", to ask if this really is the dwelling that was once on fire, and into which rushed the half-crazed man, determined to save from the flames the prized armchair of his dead mother. The house now standing was built by its present occupant on the very spot of the dwelling thus destroyed in the winter of 1853-4, and is of the same general plan. The victim was a man of legal education, well informed, but dissipated. In vain his neighbors tried to dissuade him, then an elderly man, from entering the burning building. He plunged into the fire as if to atone for all his shortcomings by one final and commanding act of self-sacrifice.

It is possible to visit Sturtevant Farm by driving up the long steep hill that leads out of Centre Harbor. Here can still be seen the room which Whittier used to occupy during the seven consecutive years of his visits, and the old four-poster in which he used to sleep, originally the property of Robert Fowle, the first Episcopal rector at Holderness. Here, too, is the desk at which Whittier wrote. Across the hall one is shown the bedchamber of Lucy Larcom, for she did literary work in this very room. At the rear of the house is a charming woodland path of shade, along which Whittier used to wander, past the little family burying ground, until he came to the great pine and its prospect over Lake Asquam.

"Alone, the level sun before;
  Below, the lake's green islands;
Beyond, in misty distance dim,
  The rugged northern highlands."

Under this spreading tree many social hours were spent with books and conversation, and one evening in 1885 Whittier surprised his friends by reading to them, in sonorous tones, his "Wood Giant,"

"Dark Titan on his Sunset Hill,
Of time and change defiant!"

Is there not something of personal reference in the fancies awakened by the great pine tree's mystic rune?

"Was it the half unconscious moan
  Of one apart and mateless,
The weariness of unshared power,
  The loneliness of greatness?"

White-spired Melvin Village, although on Lake Winnepesaukee, and the scene of "The Grave by the Lake," was probably never visited by Mr. Whittier. This is the opinion of the inhabitants, and it also helps to explain the inaccuracies of the poem, which assumes that the spot where bones of a giant were unearthed is identical with that traditionally regarded as a tribal grave of the Ossipee Indians. There is no "great mound" such as the note prefatory to the poem declares to be "at the mouth of the Melvin River." Mr. C. W. Davis of Melvin, who first visited the traditional mound forty-five years ago, has in his possession "A Gazetteer of the State of New Hampshire: by John Farmer and Jacob B. Moore: embellished with an accurate Map of the State, and several other engravings: By Abel Bowen. Concord: published by Jacob B. Moore, 1823." On page 191 of this interesting old book, under the heading "Moultonborough," occurs the following passage:

"On the line of Tuftonboro, on the shore of the lake, at the mouth of Melvin River, a gigantic skeleton was found about fifteen years since, buried in a sandy soil, apparently that of a man more than seven feet high—the jaw bones easily passing over the face of a large man. A tumulus has been discovered on a piece of newly cleared land, of the length and appearance of a human grave, and handsomely rounded with small stones, not found in this part of the country; which stones are too closely placed to be separated by striking an ordinary blow with a crowbar, and bear marks of being a composition. The Ossipee tribe of Indians once resided in this vicinity, and some years since a tree was standing in Moultonborough on which was carved in hieroglyphics the history of their expedition."

It is easy to see how a reader might assume that the first two sentences of this extract refer to the same place. As matter of fact, the skeleton was found a mile and a half from the place where the "tumulus" used to be known to the boys of the neighborhood as the Indian grave. Apparently Whittier, naturally enough, confused the two objects, and transferred the giant skeleton to the Indian burial mound.

Colonel Higginson, in his "Contemporaries," has referred to Whittier's surpassing claim to the laureateship as poet of New England. If one should need further witness to Whittier's love for New Hampshire, in particular, the published correspondence and other prose writings will be found to contain many incidental touches betokening his interest in "the wild and lonely hills and valleys" he knew so well. Always there is the tone of joy in the prospect of visiting these beloved scenes, if he is away from them, or of perfect contentment if he is face to face with their satisfying charm. To Emerson he writes: "I must go up among the New Hampshire hills, away from the sea." Perhaps the most striking single passage illustrating Whittier's transcendent regard for external nature is put into the mouth of Doctor Singletary, a character on the lines of Ian McClaren's Doctor MacLure and Whitcomb Riley's "Doc Sifers." To the good doctor heaven would be welcome, should it bear the familiar aspect of earth. He says to a friend:

"Have you not felt at times that our ordinary conceptions of heaven itself, derived from the vague hints and Oriental imagery of the Scriptures, are sadly inadequate to our human wants and hopes? How gladly would we forego the golden streets and the gates of pearl, the thrones, temples and harps, for the sunset lights of our native valleys; the wood-paths, whose moss carpets are woven with violets and wild flowers; the songs of the birds, the low of cattle, the hum of bees in the apple blossoms, the sweet, familiar voices of human life and nature! In the place of strange splendors and unknown music, should we not welcome rather whatever reminded us of the common sights and sounds of our old home?"

For a third of a century the poet of New England's life and various moods found recreation and stimulus in the sweet mid-region of New Hampshire. Here he met his friends in that intimate converse that he dearly loved. Here he talked, and read, and wrote, while the wind played its melodies through pine and maple, or rippled the bosom of the shining lake. Here he found on page and tongue the legends that the people knew, and turned them into song. Here his humor found vent in youthful sallies that vied with the spirits of his younger companions, or took shape in some impromptu rhyme that might be incorporated into the letter he was writing, or might be repeated to some laughing listener as too slight to be set down upon paper. It was of the New Hampshire hills that he said, "Nature never disappoints me," a sentence uttered more than once and of more than one place, so that it may be said to comprehend his feeling for the great world of earth and sky, which has moved so many poets to rapturous expression, as it has entered into the soul of many another man whose heart has felt although his lips are dumb.

THE WHITE MOUNTAINS

This pre-Civil War description of the White Mountains of New Hampshire presents a fine picture of the many aspects of this area including the various guest houses and hotels.

Source: <u>The New World in 1859, Being the United States and Canada, Illustrated and Described</u>. New York: C. E. Bailliere, 1859.

WHITE MOUNTAINS, NEW HAMPSHIRE.

The accomplished author of "America and the Americans" thus writes regarding this portion of the United States:—"This is one of the wildest regions in the United States. From the top of the stage we have a wide prospect over forests, pastoral valleys, ravines, and dingles; Mount Lafayette rising before us in solemn majesty, and behind us, far as the eye can reach, an undulating country, stretching away towards the frontiers of Canada. For the first 3 miles the drive lies through a tangled wood, and up an ascent so steep that our team occasionally pauses. The road is so narrow that the trees touch the carriage on both sides at the same time, and so rough that passengers hold on firmly for their lives; yet the coachman drives his six in hand with the utmost ease and skill."

During nine or ten months of the year, the summits of the mountains are covered with snow and ice, giving them a bright and dazzling appearance. On every side are long and winding gullies, deepening in their descent to the plain below.

These mountains are situated in the county of Coos, in the N. part of the State. They extend about 20 miles, from S. W. to N. E., and are the more elevated parts of a range extending many miles in that direction. Their base is about 10 miles broad, and are the highest in New England; and, if we except the Rocky Mountains, and one or two peaks in North Carolina, they are the most lofty of any in the United States.

Although these mountains are 65 miles distant from the ocean, their snow-white summits are distinctly visible, in good weather, more than 50 miles from shore. Their appearance, at that distance, is that of a silvery cloud skirting the horizon.

The names here given are those generally appropriated to the different summits: *Mount Washington* is known by its superior elevation, and by its being the southern of the three highest peaks. *Mount Adams* is known by its sharp, terminating peak, and being the north of Washington. *Jefferson* is situated between these two. *Madison* is the eastern peak of the range. *Monroe* is the first to the south of Washington. *Franklin* is the second south, and is known by its level surface. *Lafayette* is known by its conical shape, and being the third south of Washington. The ascent to the summits of these mountains, though fatiguing, is not dangerous; and the visitant is richly rewarded for his labour and curiosity. In passing from the Notch to the highest summit, the traveller crosses the summits of Mounts Lafayette, Franklin, and Monroe. In accomplishing this, he must pass through a forest, and cross several ravines. These are neither wide nor deep, nor are they discovered at a great distance; for the trees fill them up exactly even with the mountain on each side, and their branches interlock with each other in such a manner that it is very difficult to pass through them, and they are so stiff and thick as almost to support a man's weight. After crossing Mount Franklin, you pass over the eastern pinnacle of Mount Monroe, and soon find yourself on a plain of some extent, at the foot of Mount Washington. Here is a fine resting-place, on the margin of a beautiful sheet of water, of an oval form, covering about three-fourths of an acre. The waters are pleasant to the taste, and deep. Not a living creature is to be seen in the waters at this height on the hills; nor does vegetation grow in or around them, to obscure the clear rocky or gravelly bottom on which they rest. A small spring discharges itself into this pond, at its south-east angle. Another pond, of about two-thirds its size, lies north-west of this. Directly before you, the pinnacle of Mount Washington rises with majestic grandeur, like an immense pyramid, or some vast kremlin, in this magnificent city of mountains. The pinnacle is elevated about 1500 feet above the plain, and is composed principally of huge rocks of granite and gneiss, piled together, presenting a variety of colours and forms. The ascent is made on horseback.

In ascending, you must pass enormous masses of loose stone; but a ride of half an hour will generally carry you to the summit. The view from this point is wonderfully grand and picturesque. Innumerable mountains, lakes, ponds, rivers, towns, and villages meet the delighted eye, and the dim Atlantic stretches its waters along the eastern horizon. To the north is seen the lofty summits of Adams and Jefferson; and to the east, a little detached from the range, supported on the north by a high ridge, which extends to Mount Jefferson; on the north-east by a large grassy plain, terminating in a vast spur, extending far away in that direction; east, by a promontory, which breaks off abruptly at St. Anthony's Nose; south and south-east by a grassy plain, in summer, of more than 40 acres. At the south-eastern extremity of this plain a ridge commences, which slopes gracefully away towards the vale of the Saco, upon which, at short distances from each other, arise rocks, resembling in some places, towers; in others, representing the various orders of architecture.

The above house stands upon a spot which will ever remain memorable in the history of the White Mountains, as having been the scene of a fearful calamity which overtook a family named Willey, residing there, who were all buried beneath an avalanche, or slide, from the mountain, which occurred during the year 1826, a year remarkable for a great flood in these mountain regions.

Leaving Willey House, the tourist, who is desirous of ascending higher, will find himself in the vicinity of the "Notch," as it is called.

"The *Notch of the White Mountains* is a phrase appropriated to a very narrow defile, extending two miles in length, between two huge cliffs, apparently rent asunder by some vast convulsion of nature, probably that of the deluge.

"The scenery at this place is exceedingly beautiful and grand. About half a mile from the entrance of the chasm is seen a most beautiful cascade, issuing from a mountain on the right, about 800 feet above the subjacent valley, and about two miles distant. The stream passes over a series of rocks, almost perpendicular, with a course so little broken as to preserve the appearance of a uniform current, and yet so far disturbed as to be perfectly white. This beautiful stream, which passes down a stupendous precipice, is called by Dwight the *Silver Cascade*." It is probably one of the most beautiful in the world, and has been thus described:—

"The stream is scanty, but its course from among the deep forest, whence its springs issue into light, is one of singular beauty. Buried beneath the lofty precipice of the gorge, after ascending through *Pulpit Rock*, by the side of the turbulent torrent of the Saco, the ear is suddenly saluted by the soft dashings of the sweetest of cascades; and a glance upward reveals its silver streams issuing from the loftiest crests of the mountain, and leaping from crag to crag. It is a beautiful vision in the midst of the wildest and most dreary scenery."

Mount Washington House, capable of accommodating 100 guests, is situated about 4 miles from the *Notch*.

The Notch House is at the head of the Saco River, and about 9 miles from the top of Mount Washington.

The Willey House, alluded to above, is about 2 miles below the Notch.

The Crawford House, in the valley of the Saco, is about 8 miles below the Notch, these, together with the

Glen House, will be found in every respect desirable, for stopping at. Particulars of *Tip-Top House* will be found on next page.

As already explained, Mount Washington forms the highest of the range of the White Mountains, 6234 feet above the sea.

We present above, a sketch made from a photograph taken of the highest point of Mount Washington, known by travellers as "Tip-Top House," to attain to which is the ambition of all tourists who make the attempt to climb to the apex of the highest of the range in this region of "the mountain and the flood."

Tip-Top House is a rude built inn erected under most difficult circumstances, and not without great risk of life and property.

In Tip-Top House, tourists can be accommodated all night, so that any who are desirous of witnessing the setting of the sun, and being up in time for sunrise next morning, can accomplish both, by ascending in the afternoon, staying there all night, and returning next morning. Those who try the experiment, if favoured with a clear morning, will be certain to be repaid for their trouble.

Regarding the view from the summit of this dizzy height, we quote:—

"If the day be clear, a view is afforded unequalled perhaps on the eastern side of the North American continent. Around you are confused masses of mountains, bearing the appearance of a sea of molten lava suddenly cooled whilst its ponderous waves were yet in commotion. On the S. E. horizon gleams a rim of silver light—it is the Atlantic Ocean, 65 miles distant, laving the shores of Maine. Lakes of all sizes, from Lake Winnipiseogee to mere mountain ponds, and mountains beneath you, gleam misty and wide. Far off in the N. E. is Mount Katahdin. In the western horizon are the Green Mountains of Vermont, while the space is filled up with every kind of landscape—mountain and hill, plain and valley, lake and river."

It would be vain in us to attempt a description of the varied wonders which here astonish and delight the beholder. To those who have visited these mountains, our description would be tame and uninteresting; and he who has never ascended their hoary summits cannot realize the extent and magnificence of the scene. These mountains are decidedly of primitive formation. Nothing of volcanic origin has ever yet been discovered, on the most diligent research. They have for ages, probably, exhibited the same unvarying aspect. No minerals are here found of much rarity or value. The rock which most abounds is schistose, intermixed with greenstone, mica, granite, and gneiss.

There are several routes to this highland district; amongst the principal, and those which will please the tourist best, we name from Portland, Maine, per Eastern Railroad, or from Boston to Plymouth, thence per coach to the Flume House, thence through Franconia Notch—about 150 miles. Another route, and said to be the finest, is via Lake Winnipiseogee, 180 miles. Proceed from Boston per Boston and Maine and Cocheco Railroad. (See Winnipiseogee Lake, N. H.)

NEW HAMPSHIRE IN THE 20TH CENTURY

The following description indicates the financial structure of the state, the condition of industry and agriculture, the government, education, charitable institutions, and social conditions. Brief historical sketches are presented to better illustrate the early twentieth century conditions.

Source: Frank B. Sanborn. <u>New Hampshire. An Epitome of Popular Government</u>. Boston and New York: Houghton, Mifflin and Company, 1904, pp. 314-338.

NEW HAMPSHIRE IN THE TWENTIETH CENTURY

THE close of the Civil War found New Hampshire very deeply in debt. She had mustered in more than 30,000 soldiers and sailors during the four years; thousands of them had left their bones in the region where slavery had prevailed, or had reached home broken in health and incapable of self-support; a few had deserted their colors and taken refuge in Canada, or remained at the South. The state expenses, which in the year before the war had been but $175,000, were in its last year nearly $4,000,000; while the taxes, on a diminished population, had gone up from less than $200,000 to nearly a million. The state debt, merely nominal before the war, was now $4,000,000, while the town and county debts were nearly thrice that sum. The valuation of property had nominally increased, because of the inflation and depreciation of the currency, but the actual value of the property was less than in 1861. All this might seem to betoken adversity, but in fact the increase in the earning power of the people soon made good the losses of property. Farms were less profitable than formerly, but manufacturing industry had gained greatly, and the throng of citizens from other States and countries to enjoy a few months' rest among the hills was every year growing larger. In 1875 this was estimated to bring into the State between $2,500,000 and $3,000,000 yearly, exclusive of the large sum paid for railway travel by the pleasure-seekers. Even in 1862, the English novelist, Anthony Trollope, said that the White Mountain district " contained mountain scenery superior to much that is yearly crowded by tourists in Europe, was reached with ease by railways and stage-coaches, and dotted with huge hotels, almost as thickly as they lie in Switzerland." Since then the facilities for travel and residence there, and among the regions of the lower mountains and the attractive lakes and river-banks and the seashore resorts, have more than doubled. This summer population has extended itself into earlier and later seasons, and there is even a considerable resort of visitors during the severe but wholesome winters. Consequently, the farms are less frequently abandoned, and when this happens, they are often bought by residents for the summer and autumn.

Under a fluctuating and locally variable system of valuation for local taxation, it is difficult to say what is the actual value of property in the State ; but the increase since the Civil War may be indicated by a few comparisons. In 1864, at the depth of depression made by the war, the reported valuation was only $129,856,167; twenty years after, it had nearly doubled, — $227,914,613. In the year 1900 it appeared rather less, — $212,687,051, and in 1902 was $350,000 larger. But other forms of property, not subject to local taxation, such as savings-bank deposits, railroad and insurance companies, and the capital of banks of discount and loan companies, had much increased, while the state debt, which was $4,000,000 at the end of the war, had fallen to $1,000,000. The town and county debts still exceed $10,000,000, and the total of state and local taxation reaches nearly $5,000,000; the state expenses, which in 1860 were less than $180,000, now exceed $460,000 annually. The special county expenses for prisoners and the poor are large, in addition to what the State pays for those classes, — exceeding $500,000 yearly. The total outlay by State, counties, and towns for charities and correctional services must exceed $600,000 annually, and the outlay in private charity would bring the total beyond $1,000,000.

These figures indicate, what is well known, that the system of public and private charity has been much extended and developed, in consequence of the great change from a rural population, incidentally engaged in small manufactures, to a population more devoted to the great manufactures, to railroad service, and the care of large estates. This change has brought into New Hampshire a class of recent immigrants and their children, from several European countries and from Canada, whose families make larger and larger demands on the charity of the public, and that of local and religious societies. Even before the Civil War, this change had led to the introduction of county almshouses and the limitation of ancient pauper settlements, instead of the older method of local relief in each township. But at that time not more than one in twenty of the New Hampshire people was foreign-born, while now the proportion is at least one in four. The change from farming to manufacturing industry is less marked, but more general. The number of farms reported in 1850 and in 1900 was nearly the same (29,229 and 29,324), but the number of acres had increased in the half-century more than 200,000, showing there were more great farms. But the improved acres fell from 2,251,488 to 1,076,879, — showing that more than a million acres, cultivated in 1850, had gone back to pasturage and woodland in 1900. The farm property had increased in value about 29 per cent., the value of farm products remaining much the same. But when we turn to the manufactures, a great increase is seen in the half-century. The capital employed and the value of the product were more than five times as much in 1900 as in 1850; the wages paid were between four and five times as much; while the average number of wage-earners grew from 27,092 to 72,612. Manufacturing has thus become the leading interest of the State, while before the war, farming was much the foremost interest. It is true that a tenth part of this manufacturing deals with products of the improved or unimproved land in the farms, and employs thousands of persons in outdoor labor; but the greater part of the persons employed are in large factories or workshops, and the tendency is to concentrate them in cities more and more. This gives the matter a social and political importance it would not otherwise have, since it establishes a conflict of interests between the cities or larger towns and the scattered population of the small towns. It also accumulates the people of foreign birth and parentage in a comparatively small number of municipalities, and throws upon those the burdens induced by illiteracy, unsanitary habits, and religious divisions, from which the majority of the towns are measurably free.

Naturally, the persons of foreign parentage, whether born abroad or in the State, are more likely to be children and youth than adults and voting citizens. Thus, of 110,895 persons of school age in New Hampshire in 1900, 52,676 were of foreign parentage, — nearly half. But of the voting age, out of 130,648 men, only 48,265, or a little more than one third, were of foreign parentage. Yet of these 9039 were illiterate, — almost one in five; while of the 82,383 men of native parentage, only 1256, or one in 66, were illiterate.[1]

[1] In 1820, when the population was 244,161, the occupations of 62,141 inhabitants were reported; of whom more than five sixths

Among the whole population in 1900 (411,588), only 243,300 were of native parentage, while (52,384) were in agriculture, not quite one seventh (8699) in manufactures, and a little more than one sixtieth (1058) in commerce. Eighty years later, the population having increased to 411,588, the number of occupations reported was more than twice as great as in 1820, — of whom those on manufactures were more than 77,000, including owners of the 4671 establishments; while, although the number of farms had much increased since 1820, only about 50,000 were engaged in agriculture. This includes, of course, many of those persons who are also engaged in forestry and lumbering; since by estimate 5200 square miles, out of 9005 of the land surface, are said to be in woodland, while the farms reported are only 5640 square miles. A comparison of these figures will show that at least 1500 square miles are both covered with wood and included in the farms. The forest products rated as farm products are not given in the census tables, but must have exceeded $500,000, or an average of $20 for each of the 30,000 farms. The reported "forest products" were valued in 1899 at about $2,300,000.

In the first census taken after the Civil War, the whole number reported in occupations was 120,568; of these, the number in manufactures was 46,533, in agriculture 46,573, in professional and personal service, 18,528, in trade and transportation, 8514. Here, as the women in agriculture reported were but 11, it is plain that the number 46,573 is too small; since every farm of the 29,642 counted, must have had at least one woman, by average; while of the personal service women (9707), at least 1000 must have been domestics on farms. It is therefore probable that the real aggregate engaged in agriculture was not less than 77,000 out of 151,000 who should have been reported. In 1900, the number reckoned on the same basis was perhaps 70,000, — the farm labor being done by machinery and in creameries, etc., off the farms, to a much greater extent than thirty years before. Probably, then, out of some 200,000 whose occupations should have been reported in 1900, a little more than one third were agricultural, where, eighty years before, five sixths were so.

In the valuation and debt tables of General Walker's census

168,290 were either foreign-born (88,074) or of foreign parentage born here. Thirty years before, in a population not quite 100,000 less (318,300), the foreign-born were but 29,611, and those of foreign parentage born here, 44,592. Thus in one generation the foreign-born in New Hampshire have trebled, and those of foreign parentage considerably more than doubled, — from 72,203, increasing to 168,290. In six cities, Berlin, Concord, Keene, Manchester, Nashua, and Dover, where manufactures are the leading interest, more than 82,000 are of foreign parentage, while only a little more than 49,000 are of native stock.

To preserve some ratio to the increase of urban inhabitants, and yet to retain political power, at least nominally, in the rural towns and larger villages, the State Constitution has been several times slightly amended, and provision is now made that the additional representation due to increase of population shall be one for every 1200 inhabitants;

of 1870, the New Hampshire figures are curious, and show the influence of the Civil War in swelling taxation and inflating the currency. He estimated the "true" valuation of property in the State at $252,624,000, as against $156,311,000 in 1860, and $103,653,000 in 1850. But the taxation, general and local, which was but $1,261,806 in 1860, had swollen to $3,255,793 in 1870; and the public debt (very small before the war) had grown to $11,153,373, or $35 *per capita* for every man, woman, and child; besides their share of the national debt, which was then $2,406,562, — or $7.50 *per capita*. That New Hampshire has reached her present prosperity in the face of such facts shows the vigor of her people, as well as the general progress of the nation.

while every town or ward having 600 shall have one representative, and towns of smaller size shall be represented as often in twelve years as their population bears a ratio to 600. Thus a town of 100 will have a representative once in six years, and one of 500, five years in twelve.

The Senate remains fixed at twenty-four members, and the Council at five. As an additional check on illiteracy in the mass of the people, the new amendments provide for reading and writing as a qualification for voting; and it will be lawful hereafter to tax franchises as well as property. A general valuation by town inventories is to be made every five years. More important in theory, and perhaps to be made operative in practice, is a new provision denouncing "monopolies and conspiracies which tend to hinder or destroy free and fair competition;" and declaring that "the size and functions of all corporations should be so limited and regulated as to prohibit fictitious capitalization; and provisions should be made for the supervision and government thereof."

This is an intimation that the recent control of legislation and appointments in New Hampshire, alleged to reside in a single corporation (the Boston and Maine Railroad), will not be allowed to grow into a permanent feature of the government. It is a significant change in the state policy that while in the years about 1840, when the first railroads were building, the legislation was unfriendly, and many evils were predicted, should corporations succeed in establishing themselves firmly in New Hampshire, now the legislation and administration have for many years been favorable to corporations of all kinds. Some of the evils prophesied are beginning to be feared again, and hence the warning sections of the amended Constitution.

Another great change has occurred regarding the laws to regulate the sale of liquor. New Hampshire was one of the first States to follow the example of Maine and Massachusetts in enacting prohibition of such sales, except for medical and mechanical uses; and the strictness of these laws was kept up in name long after their violation was frequent in fact. At last, after a referendum vote on the question, indicating majorities for a license system, such as had long prevailed before 1855, the legislature of 1902 passed a liberal licensing act, which is now on trial, with very different results in different communities. It will bring a considerable revenue, but will perhaps be accompanied, as a like system has been in Massachusetts, by a large increase in vice and crime.

So far as education is a barrier to crime, New Hampshire may be said to be now better protected than ever. The teaching of children in the common schools is carried farther and improved in its methods; while the higher education of boys and girls is endowed and promoted much better than formerly. Dartmouth College was never so much frequented by students as for the past five years, nor ever so well prepared to carry on their instruction. Technical education has been undertaken by the State at an agricultural college in Durham, endowed by a wealthy citizen of that small town; and the ancient Academy at Exeter, a few miles farther south, has greatly enlarged its buildings, resources, and number of students. It now gives a more advanced education than Dartmouth did in the days of Webster, Chase, and Choate, and to twice as many young men. The higher education of girls is provided for in numerous seminaries, high schools, and academies; many of the older schools of that name having now been opened to the public as local high schools. Public libraries, also a wonderful aid and stimulus to education, are everywhere gaining both in number and excellence, maintained as public gifts, but more frequently owing their existence to private endowment. Of late the State has encouraged the formation of free libraries by a small grant in aid. Their whole number at last accounts was 230, and they were established in 225 cities and towns.

The average length of the school year in days has been doubled in New Hampshire since 1870, being then but 70 days, and in 1902 140 days. The expenditure for public and private schools has also more than doubled, being less than $450,000 in 1870, and now more than $1,100,000. The whole enrollment of pupils in 1902 was 78,793, of whom a little more than one seventh were in private schools. The estimated value of all the public school property is from $4,000,000 to $6,000,000, and if the private school and college property is added, the total would exceed $6,000,000. The State itself carries on the education of its blind, deaf, and feeble-minded children, chiefly at establishments in Massachusetts; and has recently cared for the maintenance of pauper children in families at the expense of the several counties, — all this under the direction of an efficient Board of State Charities. A State Conference of Charities aids in this work.

The development of a system of public charities in a small State, that till forty years ago was mainly rural, must naturally be very unlike the same in States of dense population and great wealth. In one respect, the care of the insane, New Hampshire has been well abreast of the advancing movement. Its one hospital for the treatment of acute cases and the restraint and comfort of the chronic, built at Concord more than sixty years since, has been fortunate in the skill, experience, and long service of its management. It still enjoys the services of a veteran trustee, Mr. Walker (a descendant of the founder of Rumford, Rev. Timothy Walker), who has been for more than half a century in office. The two superintendents, father and son, Drs. J. P. and C. P. Bancroft, have successively directed its medical service for as long a period, and have added to its wards and improved its classification, with a steady regard to humanity and good sense not always found in such establishments, where vague theory and costly experiment have too often gone hand in hand, with little benefit to the patients or the public.

This New Hampshire State Hospital was originally founded by the donations of individuals combining with a state appropriation, and its Board of Trustees then contained an equal number representing the private donors and the State. Recently the private donors withdrew from the board at the request of the legislature, with the privilege of withdrawing their gifts also; but though withdrawing from representation on the board, they chose not to remove their donations. The State then assumed entire control of the hospital, as well as exclusive ownership of the property. Somewhat later the whole question of state ownership was raised by the legislature of 1899, and a resolution passed requesting an opinion from the Supreme Court, whether, as owner of the hospital and its funds, the State's title is a fee simple or "charged with trust." The court decided that the State possesses absolute ownership with complete control of the property.

When the question of public care for the insane was first agitated, seventy years ago, an impetus given to the general interest by the activity of many benevolent persons in different counties led to considerable private donations, which have been carefully preserved. The income from this source has defrayed the expense of many patients with moderate means, who would otherwise have been objects of public charity. These funds now amount to $300,000. It is certain that the position of this State Hospital is unique, in that it has such large funds well invested, the income of which aids those who pay all they can toward their support, rather than become wholly a public charge.

In reviewing the history of this hospital, the first of the distinctly state establishments for the dependent classes (the State Prison, which was earlier organized upon a sound principle, being for delinquents), one is struck with the early and constant interest taken in its foundation and management by the leading citizens of the State. It was first recommended by Governor Dinsmoor in 1832, strongly urged for years by the leading physicians and professional men, and actually opened in 1842, with room for 100 patients, out of a supposed insane population in New Hampshire of 500. On its board of management have served governors, senators, and congressmen, and for a time President Pierce, before he was chosen to the presidency. It has pursued a steady policy, always a little in advance of professional opinion in the country at large, and has secured large endowment from citizens of the State, — a good indication of its high character. At present it has room for some 500 patients, in buildings much less costly than most of such hospitals, and yet quite equal to others in comfort and classification of inmates. It has only of late been exclusively a state establishment, subject to the vicissitudes of party politics; but its trustees have drawn its resources from private citizens, from towns, counties, and the State, — its receipts from the taxpayers being now between $50,000 and $60,000 a year, in an outlay of some $200,000. This has relieved it from the embarrassing dependence on votes of the legislature, which often restrict the efficiency of such hospitals, and may yet do so there under the new policy.

There can be no strict separation between the dependent insane and the mass of the public poor, for of all the causes of permanent pauperism in New England, insanity is one of the largest and most constant. The poor laws of New Hampshire were inherited from England, but modified by the needs of the colonists, and at first left the support of the poor wholly to the towns. Paupers were few during the first two centuries, much of the distress occurring being relieved by neighborly aid without the stigma of pauperism attaching to the recipients. But before 1843, with the growth of manufactures inviting a foreign immigration, the number and cost of the public poor began to increase, showing itself first in the county expenses for such as had no lawful "settlement" in any town. The careful and frugal state authorities in 1843 required a return from the ten counties — Belknap and Carroll having been recently organized — for the five years, 1839-43, of the county cost of the unsettled poor; and it appeared that in 1838-39 this did not exceed $10,000. In 1842 it had grown to be nearly $30,000, — the manufacturing county of Hillsborough alone expending $7000, or two thirds of what the whole State paid a few years earlier. At that time (1842-43), the state population being about 300,000, the towns did not pay more than $80,000 for their poor, and the whole cost could not have exceeded $120,000. In 1902, the population having reached 420,000, the towns still paid $148,000 for outdoor relief, to which the counties added $61,000, while the indoor relief, or almshouse cost, by the counties, was $135,000. This shows a total of nearly $350,000, where sixty years earlier little more than a third had sufficed; and by that time (1902) at least half the public poor were of foreign parentage, and a third of them foreign-born. Great differences exist among the counties in this respect. Those with a rural population have fewer indoor poor, and those having a manufacturing population (notably Hillsborough) have many poor, and among them a disproportionate number of the insane. Thus in 1892 Hillsborough, with less than 300 inmates of its new and well-built county almshouse at Grasmere, near Manchester, had more of the foreign-born than of natives, and more than half were rated either insane or idiotic; while

Carroll, in the mountain region, had only one in nine of foreign birth, and less than one in three who were insane. Of the foreign-born, about two thirds are Irish, one fifth Canadian French, and one tenth British. Of the prison population, an average of less than 500, about the same ratio are Canadian, but the other foreign-born are less in proportion.

Intermediate between the almshouses and the insane hospital and prisons are three other establishments, none very large, — the Industrial School at Manchester, founded in 1855 for young offenders, male and female; the Orphan Asylum at Franklin, on the farm of Daniel Webster; and the new school for the feeble-minded at Laconia, containing in all three less than 500 children and youths. Only the first and last are maintained by the State, the Orphan Asylum being mainly supported by private funds and the income of gifts. Each in its way, these are excellent establishments; the last named is a model for thorough care and sanitation, combined with frugality, and the other two have the same general character.

The county almshouses (the tenth having been rebuilt since it burned down) have not had the same good reputation as the State Charities; but they have been much improved in the past ten years, and are not likely to fall back into the condition of most poorhouses before the National Conference of Charities, now for thirty years in existence, raised their standard in the nation at large. In New Hampshire the State Conference of Charities has done much to remedy the neglects from ignorance, and a few abuses. The character of the people is fundamentally charitable, and a guaranty against serious mismanagement.

In penitentiary discipline, New Hampshire was one of the first States to adopt modern ideas, under the direction of the Pilsbury family, who for three generations managed prisons on the Auburn plan in Connecticut and New York, as well as in their native State. It was the most eminent of these disciplinarians, Amos Pilsbury, who trained in his youth that man of genius, Mr. Brockway of Connecticut, to whom the world owes the most effective system for young felons now in use at Elmira and other reformatory prisons. The small State Prison at Concord no longer stands in the front rank, yet is of fair reputation, and a useful adjunct to the correctional system of county prisons. A workhouse for misdemeanants is much needed for those now sentenced to almshouses. The yearly cost of the prison system may be estimated at $60,000. The judiciary of the State stood high when its justices were country gentlemen and clergymen, for the most part; it rose to eminence in its decisions, when the great lawyers of the older counties, Mason, Plumer, Livermore, Smith, Webster, Sullivan, Woodbury, Richardson, etc., adorned the bar and bench, before 1830. It has well maintained its standard since, but not relatively, perhaps, though its decisions have seldom been overruled since the Dartmouth College case in 1817. In one marked instance, twenty-five years later, the state court declined to modify its decision when reversed by the national Supreme Court, and that august body afterward took the New Hampshire view of the case, when Judge Woodbury had succeeded to Story's place on the bench.

Whether the influence of wealth, aggregated in railroads and other corporations, has affected the judiciary in New Hampshire, as it occasionally does in Vermont and New York, is a question; but there can be no doubt that the State has suffered in its political morals by the growth of corporations. The governors in 1840-45 were wise in their warnings against endowing such aggregations of wealth with peculiar privileges, not granted to partnerships or individuals. Governor Hubbard, an eminent lawyer, and originally a Federalist, in his addresses to the legislature (1842-43), expressed opinions too little regarded of late, even in communities where property is distributed so equally as it has been in New Hampshire and Vermont. He said: —

"The great design in the constitution of free political communities is, to protect the weak from the encroachments of the strong; to defend the impotent from the influence of power, and to sustain the whole people in the enjoyment of their liberty and equality. The principle that individual property shall not be taken, except for public use, is, in a republic, the surest guaranty of individual independence. The tendency of our legislation is to disregard individual rights. The authority to establish private corporations cannot give to the representative body of the people any new power over the private rights of individuals. Highways are the work of public corporations, and are wholly distinguishable, in their character, use, and purpose, from ways wrought by individuals or private corporations. These are constructed for private benefit, with private means; of this description are the railroads. The public are shut out from a participation in their government and direction. Upon such a corporation power cannot be conferred to take individual property for its use without the owner's consent."

This exact issue, being raised in Governor Hubbard's time, was then decided in accordance with his view; but now other doctrines seem to prevail for what are called "semi-public" corporations, like railroads, whether for steam or electric locomotion. And it has been found that, though the public may be "shut out from participation in the direction of railroads," railroads are not shut out from the direction of government. They have had too much influence for thirty years in aiding or thwarting the political fortunes of the ambitious; and they seem to have taken advantage of the growing evil of vote-buying, to influence the choice of legislators and their action when chosen. A perception of this doubtless gave occasion for an amendment to the State Constitution adopted in 1903. In the years of Governor Steele, who followed Hubbard (1844–45), he expressed similar opinions more pointedly. He was a "poor white" from North Carolina, who had migrated to Peterborough, and by his mechanic skill and financial faculty made himself independent in fortune, as he naturally was in mind. When governor he said (1844): —

"I know of no valid reason why associated wealth in any form should enjoy by law privileges or exemptions which are denied to partnerships or individuals."

(1845.) "The granting to combined wealth of exclusive privileges or immunities would, ere long, raise the grantees above the grantors; and corporate bodies would soon usurp the power, without possessing the dignity or personal responsibility of the landed and titled aristocracy of Europe. . . . Grant protection to all who ask it, and in the end many sections of our country, if not all, will present the sad spectacle of inordinate wealth on the one hand, and squalid poverty on the other, — *of a people bought with and scrambling after their own money: a Congress changed into a board of assessors*, and the Executive Department presided over by the man who promises most to his own supporters."

There are many who think that we have already attained the position thus depicted by this democratic moralist. He was then considering the existing tariff, which was but moderate in its taxation of the consumer for the enrichment of the manufacturer, compared with the rates now existing. These rates New Hampshire before the Civil War would have resisted by great majorities; now she seems to favor them.

No doubt the disproportion between wealth and poverty in the State increases, not only among those resident the whole year, but among the rich families from other States (who buy large tracts and reside on some corner of them for a few months in the summer) and their laborers and dependents. One such estate, of enormous extent for New Hampshire, exists on the borders of Sullivan and Grafton counties, devoted to a park for beasts of the chase. It was purchased about 1870 by the late Austin Corbin of New York, contains 25,000 acres, and has cost half a million. Among its wild denizens are 150 buffaloes, 300 wild boars, twenty or thirty moose, and thousands of smaller beasts and birds; while a few families of men and women care for the interests involved. As a museum of natural history and a forest preserve, this adds to the attractions of the State. Other tracts of less extent, but still large, are owned by rich men or by companies for the supply of wood-paper, or other uses of the timbered regions in the mountain district. In the wood-pulp manufacture alone, twenty proprietors (firms or individuals) have 29 establishments, with a capital valued at more than $8,000,000 and employing nearly 2500 men and women, whose annual product exceeds $1,250,000. Including this new interest, the whole value of the timber and wood-working capital is $20,000,000, vested in 5800 establishments, great and small, and employing 6600 hands, chiefly men. The annual product of this varied industry is placed at $17,000,000, or nearly as much as the capital invested, which capital has increased by ten millions in twelve years. Impelled by this growing exploitation of the forests, the State has created an intelligent forestry commission, whose report indicates what is doing to destroy, and what may be done to preserve, this ornament and treasure of New Hampshire. Its first report declares that the area in the State now covered with foliage, including much that has no present value, is larger than at any time since 1850; and that, though valuable timber and fuel have been cut off and many forest fires occur, there has been no perceptible decrease of rainfall, or loss of water power, — the latter being the greatest single resource of New Hampshire, especially since the applications of electricity to industry. This is more encouraging than there was reason to expect, and the measures proposed to reforest the denuded regions will perhaps keep good this condition.

It is shown that the capital invested in "summer property" (hotels, boarding-houses, pleasure-boats, and carriages, etc.) is but little greater than in the wood-pulp industry, though employing many more persons, and providing for 175,000 guests in an average year. Out of 235 towns in the State, 204 share in this interest. With a capital of $10,500,000, it pays $540,000 in wages to 12,350 persons, and furnishes a gross income to railroads and transportation companies of more than $700,000. Its own gross income approaches $7,000,000, and increases in magnitude each decade. The connection between it and the railroad corporations, particularly the Boston and Maine, gives popular strength to them and to similar investments of wealth. The state government for some years past has aided the influx of summer guests by building state highways and protecting the public rights, in lakes and streams for fishing, against the encroachments of private owners.

Altogether, it may be said that the material interests of New Hampshire, and its higher civilization, as shown in education, charity, and the encouragement of literature, were never more prosperous or advancing than now. Its moral interests are somewhat imperiled by the influence of unscrupulous wealth and irresponsible poverty, developing a proletariat in the place of that historical yeomanry, whose possession of landed property gave assurance that government would not get beyond the control of families who had, as their ancestors used to say, "a stake in the country." The scale of political rectitude in state affairs has been lowered, and the purchase of voters, which fifty years ago was almost unknown, is now alleged to be a general custom. Coincident with this, the eminence of men at the head of the government, of congressmen and senators and leaders in the legislature, is less noteworthy than in the first half of the last century, — a fact illustrated by the admirable collection of portraits at Concord, in which New Hampshire excels most of the States. No men of such mark as Langdon, Plumer, and Woodbury have lately been governors; no senators have equaled Mason, Pierce, and Hale; few congressmen have ranked with Webster, Bell, Atherton, Norris, Tuck, and Wilson. The naïve remark of a country member to John Langdon, when the courtly governor, in 1810, was telling the legislative committee that "he distrusted his own ability to perform the high duties of the office," has more than once been strictly verified. "O Governor," said the encouraging rustic, "don't be afraid! it does n't take much of a man to govern New Hampshire."

Yet in the vigor of its soldiers, the enterprise of its men of affairs, and the active genius of its whole population, seeking fields of activity in other States and countries, New Hampshire is as marked as ever. Its institutions, if threatened by the sordid spirit of a too commercial age, are still supported by a courage and independence in the mass of the people, such as threw off the yoke of the Stuarts in the seventeenth, and of King George in the eighteenth century. That sturdy compound of English obstinacy, Scotch pugnacity, and Irish ingenuity, which carried the Colony, the Province, and the youthful State through its perils by land and sea, and among false brethren, yet makes the foundation of its community; and self-reliance, forged and tested in the wars and toils of three centuries, is the lasting fibre of its individual character.

BASIC FACTS

Capital City	Concord
Nickname	The Granite State
Flower	Purple Lilac
Bird	Purple Finch
Tree	White Birch
Song	*Old New Hampshire*
Entered the Union	June 21, 1788

STATISTICS*

Land Area (square miles)	9,027
Rank in Nation	44th
Population†	774,000
Rank in Nation	41st
Density per square mile	85.7
Number of Representatives in Congress	2
Capital City	Concord
Population	30,022
Rank in State	3rd
Largest City	Manchester
Population	87,754
Number of Cities and Towns over 10,000 Population‡	13
Number of Counties	10

---

* Based on 1970 census statistics compiled by the Bureau of the Census
† Estimated by Bureau of Census for July 1, 1972.
‡ Includes 3 towns over 10,000 population.

MAP OF CONGRESSIONAL DISTRICTS OF NEW HAMPSHIRE

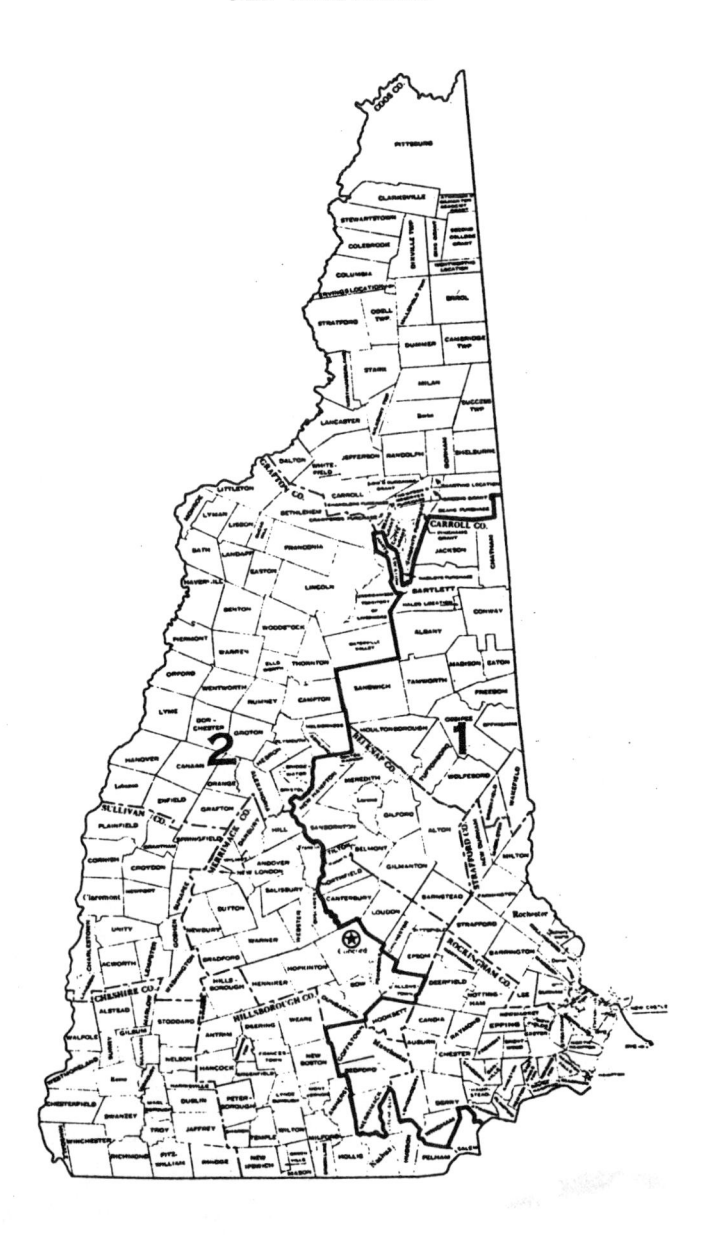

SELECTED BIBLIOGRAPHY

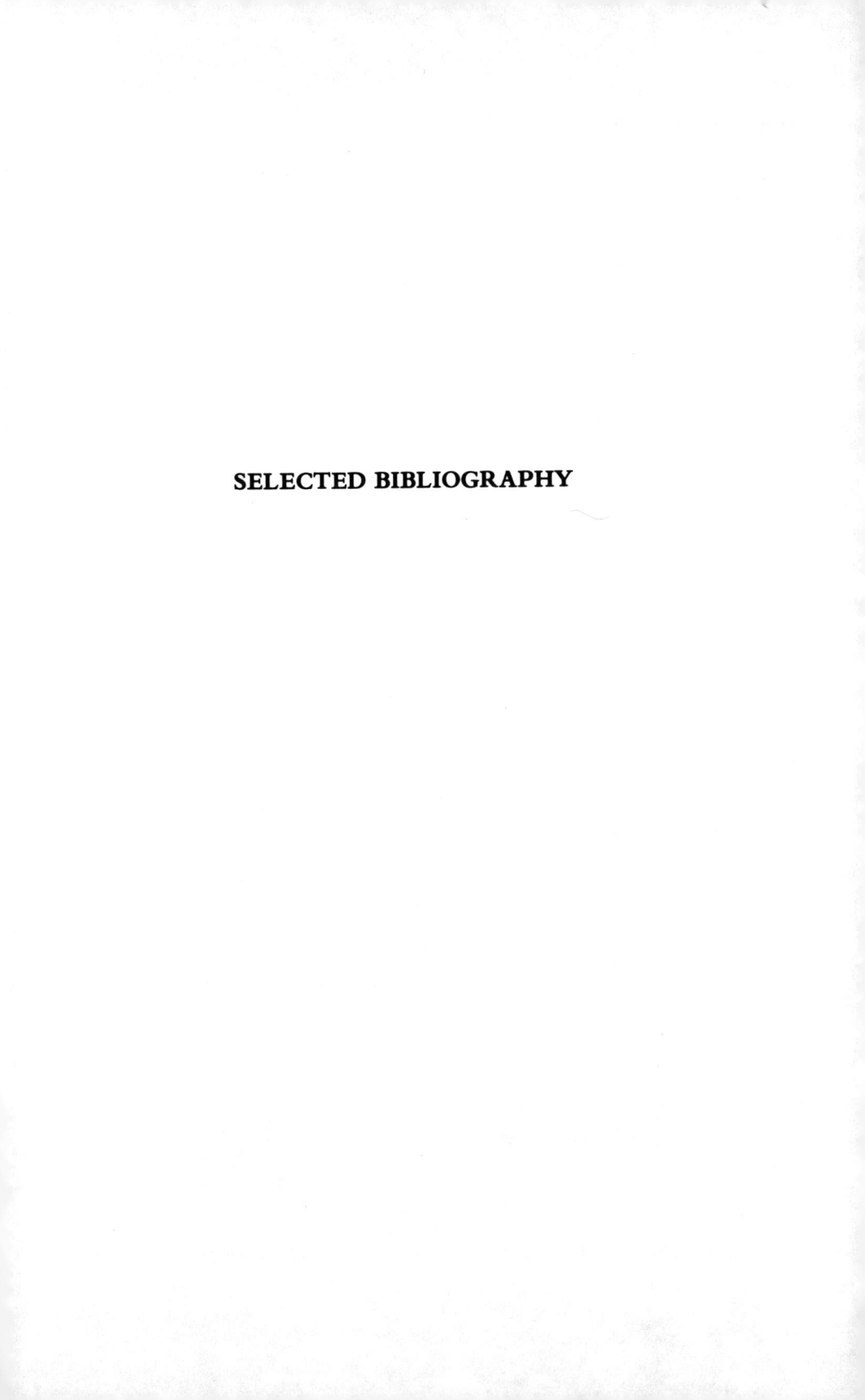

SELECTED BIBLIOGRAPHY

Belknap, Jeremy. *The History of New Hampshire*. 3 vols. Boston: Published by Bradford and Read, 1813

Browne, George Waldo. *The Story of New Hampshire*. Manchester, N. H.: Standard Book Co., Inc., 1925.

Fry, William Henry. *New Hampshire as a Royal Province*. New York: Columbia University, Longmans, Green and Company, 1908.

Hill, Ralph Nadiny. *Yankee Kingdom: Vermont and New Hampshire*. New York: Harper, 1960.

Kinney, Charles B., Jr. *Church and State: The Struggle for Separation in New Hampshire, 1630-1900*. New York: Teachers College, Columbia University, 1955.

Page, Elwin Lawrence. *Judicial Beginnings in New Hampshire, 1640-1700*. Concord: New Hampshire Historical Society, 1959.

Sanborn, Edwin David. *The History of New Hampshire*. Manchester, N. H.: J. B. Clarke, 1875.

Squires, James Duane. *The Granite State of the United States; A History of New Hampshire from 1623 to the Present*. 4 vols. New York: American Historical Company, 1956.

Stackpole, Everett Schermerhorn. *History of New Hampshire*. 5 vols. New York: The American Historical Society, 1916-18.

Upton, Richard Francis. *Revolutionary New Hampshire*. Hanover: Dartmouth College Publications, 1936.

Willey, George Franklin. *State Builders*. Manchester, N. H.: The New Hampshire Publishing Corporation, 1903.

NAME INDEX

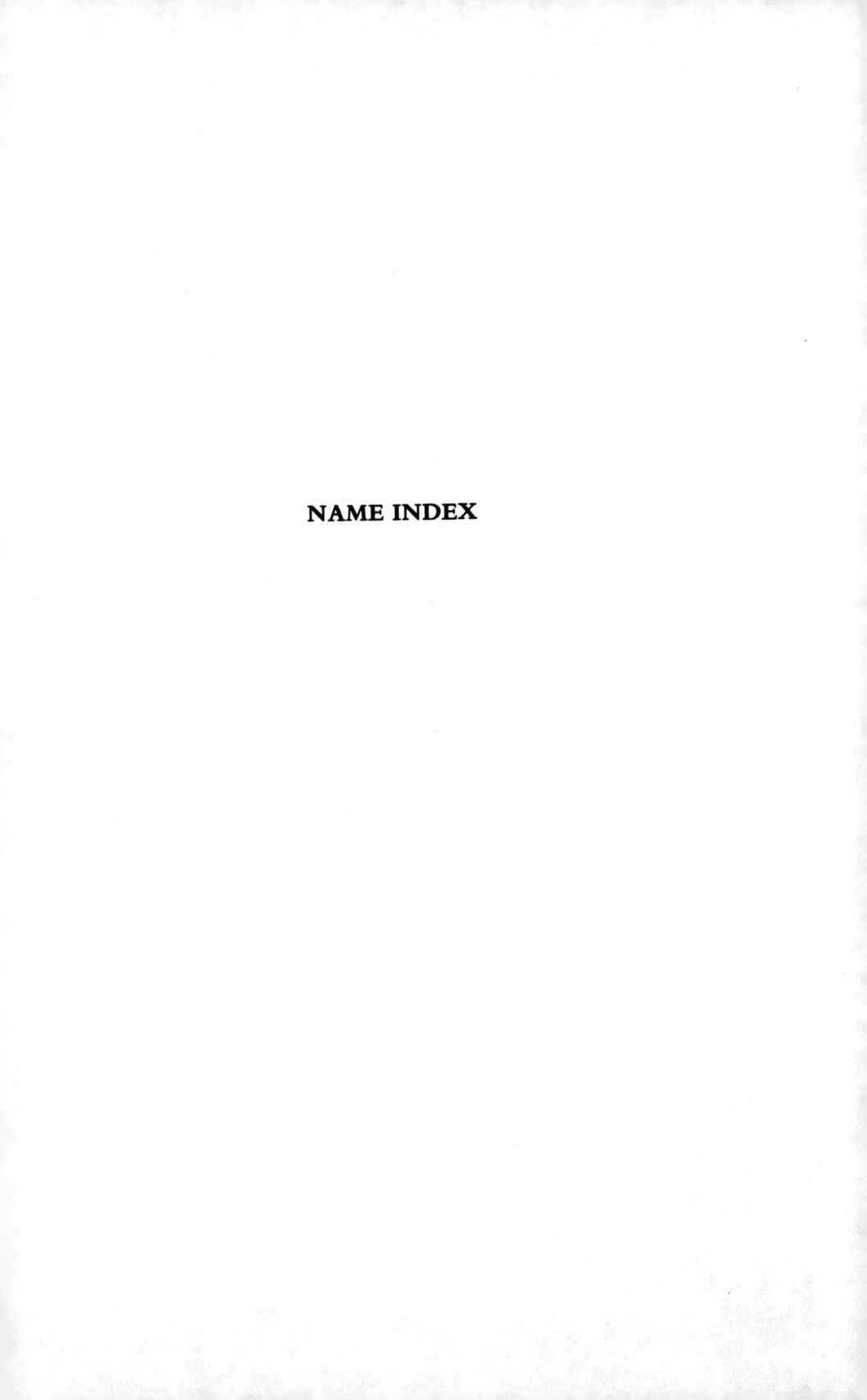

NAME INDEX

Adams, Sherman, 17
Allen, Samuel, 3, 4
Andros, Sir Edmund, 3
Arthur, Chester Alan, 13

Bachelder, Nahum Josiah, 14
Badger, William, 10
Baker, Nathaniel Bradley, 11
Barefoot, Walter, 3
Bartlett, John H., 15
Bartlett, Josiah, 7
Bass, Robert P., 15
Belcher, Jonathan, 4
Belknap, Jeremy, 10
Bell, Charles Henry, 13
Bell, Samuel, 8
Berry, Nathaniel Springer, 11
Blood, Robert O., 16
Bridges, H. Styles, 16
Brown, Albert O., 15
Brown, Fred H., 16
Burnett, William, 4
Busiel, Charles Albert, 14

Cabot, John, 1
Carroll, Charles, 10
Catt, John, 3
Champlain, Samuel de, 1
Chandler, William E., 13
Charles I, King of England, 2
Cheney, Person Colby, 13
Colby, Anthony, 11
Coote, Richard, Earl of Bellamont, 4
Coterreal, 1
Cranfield, Edward, 3
Currier, Moody, 13

Dale, Charles M., 17
Dinsmoor, Samuel, 10, 11

Dudley, Joseph, 3, 4
Dwinell, Lane, 17

Felker, Samuel D., 15
Floyd, Charles M., 14

George III, King of England, 5
Gilman, Joseph Taylor, 7
Gilmore, Joseph Albree, 12
Goodell, David Harvey, 13
Goodwin, Ichabod, 11
Gorges, Sir Ferdinando, 1
Grafton, August Henry Fitzroy, third Duke of, 5
Gregg, Hugh, 17

Haile, William, 11
Hale, Samuel Whitney, 13
Harper, Joseph Morrill, 10
Harriman, Walter, 12
Harvey, Matthew, 9
Head, Natt, 13
Hill, Isaac, 10
Hill, Willis, Earl of Hillsborough, 5
Hilton, Edward, 1
Hodges, Luther N., 17
Hubbard, Henry, 10

Jackson, Andrew, 10
Jay, John, 8
Johnson, James, 5
Johnson, Mrs. James, 5
Jordan, Chester Bradley, 14

Kennedy, John F., 17
Keyes, Henry W., 15
King, John W., 18

Landon, John, 7
Langdon, John, 8
Lincoln, Abraham, 11

Marsh, Sylvester, 12
Martin, Noah, 11
Mason, John, 1, 2, 3
Mason, Richard Tufton, 2, 3
McLane, John, 14
Metcalf, Ralph, 11
Morrill, David Lawrence, 9
Murphy, Francis P., 16

Page, John, 10
Peterson, Walter R., 18
Pierce, Benjamin, 9
Plumer, William, 8
Powell, Wesley, 17
Prescott, Benjamin Franklin, 13
Pring, Martin, 1

Quinby, Henry B., 14

Ramsdell, George Allen, 14
Rollins, Frank West, 14
Roswell, Sir Henry, 1

Sawyer, Charles Henry, 13
Shepard, Alan B., Jr., 17
Shute, Samuel, 4
Smith, Jeremiah, 8
Smith, John Butler, 14
Smyth, Frederick, 12
Spaulding, Huntley N., 16
Spaulding, Rolland N., 15
Stark, John, 9
Stearns, Onslow, 12
Steele, John Hardy, 10
Straw, Ezekiel Albert, 12
Sullivan, John, 6, 7, 9

Thomason, David, 1
Thomson, Meldrin, 19
Thornton, Matthew, 6
Tobey, Charles W., 17
Tuttle, Hiram Americas, 13

Waldron, Richard, 3
Weare, Mesteck, 6
Wentworth, Benning, 4
Wentworth, Charles Watson, Marquis of Rockingham, 5
Wentworth John, 4, 5
Wentworth, Thomas, Earl of Strafford, 5
Weston, James Adams, 12, 13
Wheelwright, Rev. John, 2
Whitefield, George, 6
William IV, King of England, 3
Williams, Jared Warner, 11
Winant, John G., 16
Woodbury, Levi, 9, 10